Near Believing

By the same author

Poetry

Public Relations
New Devil, New Parish
The Nightmarkets
Out Here (UK)
The Lovemakers, Book One, Saying all the Great Sexy Things
The Lovemakers, Book Two, Money and Nothing
The Lovemakers (UK)
The Australian Popular Songbook
Prepare the Cabin for Landing
These Things are Real

Edited

The Best Australian Poetry 2009
With the Youngsters: Group Sestinas and Group Villanelles

Fiction

Kicking in Danger

Near Believing
Selected Monologues &
Narratives 1967-2021

Alan Wearne

Edited with an Introduction by
Michelle Borzi

PUNCHER & WATTMANN

First published in 2022
Published by Puncher & Wattmann
PO Box 279
Waratah NSW 2298

info@puncherandwattmann.com

NATIONAL
LIBRARY
OF AUSTRALIA

A catologue record for this book is available from The National Library of Australia.

ISBN   9781922571298

The cover, designed by Marius Foley is a detail from a painting by Jenny Watson, *Untitled (girl in the mirror)* 1985 and is reproduced courtesy of the artist and Roslyn Oxley9 Gallery Sydney courtesy and The University of Wollongong Art Collection.

Printed by Lightning Source International

for Annie English

Like tales that were told the day before yesterday-
Wallace Stevens *The Hermitage at the Centre*

Nobody understands me & I am perfectly satisfied.
Thomas Gray on *The Progress of Poesy. A Pindaric Ode.*

If I watch them long enough I see them come together, I see them <u>placed</u>,
I see them engaged in this or that act or in this or that difficulty. How they
look and move and speak and behave, always in the setting I have found for
them, is my account of them.
Ivan Turgenev as told to Henry James

There's an old Australian bush song
Melba used to sing.
Cole Porter *Be Like the Blue Bird*

This is not meat
For little people or for fools.
Book of the Sages.
George Meredith, placed opposite Sonnet I in the
original 1862 edition of *Modern Love*

I don't know if I like it, but it's what I meant.
Vaughan Williams on his 4th Symphony

Imitate, and what is personal will eventually come despite yourself.
Jean Cocteau

So, set 'em up, Joe
I got a little story you oughta know
Johnny Mercer and Harold Arlen,
One for My Baby (and One More for the Road)

Contents

Introduction by Michelle Borzi   11

from *Poems 1967-1974*

    Saint Bartholomew Remembers Jesus Christ as an Athlete   27

    St Kilda   28

    Warburton 1910   29

    Eating Out   30

from *Out Here*

    Yes. Just   35

    Home   40

    Growing   45

    Like it's some ghost town   50

    Midnight Thru Dawn   57

from *The Nightmarkets*

    Climbing Up the Ladder of Love   63

from *The Lovemakers*

    Cross QC: Three Villanelles   83

    Roger, or Of Love and its Anger   86

    Sophie   99

    Nothing But Thunder   108

    Leo   129

from *The Great Australian Song Book*

    Down Under   133

    It's Time   134

    On the Road to Gundagai   135

    The Never Never   136

    A Brown Slouch Hat   137

    Girls on the Avenue   138

    My Old Man's a Groovy Old Man   139

    Bound for Botany Bay   140

    A World of Our Own   141

I Go to Rio 142

Bad Habits 143

Love is in the Air 144

My Home Among the Gum Trees 145

Metropolitan Poems and other poems

Chatswood: Ruth Nash Speaks 149

The God of Nope 153

Neutral Bay 158

A Portrait of Three Young High School Teachers 159

A High School Staff Room, Melbourne's Northern
          Suburbs, Winter 1977 161

Breakfast with Darky 162

They Came to Moorabbin 168

Anger Management: a South Coast Tale 179

Waitin' for the Viet Cong. 186

Operation Hendrickson 195

Near Believing 220

Press Play 243

Notes 246

Introduction

'I like raiding this country for its potential to write about. I do like the idea of being moderately uncompromising, if such a thing exists, in the Australian potential of my poetry'.[1] That comment by Alan Wearne in 2011 is a characteristic one. In his six published books of poetry, he has found a poetic plainsong among the particulars and localities of middle-class Australian suburbia, imaginatively charting a pageant of conversational vernacular from suburban and urban cultures, and sub-cultures. The poems predominantly explore the 1950s to the 1980s, but the broad span is from the early to the late twentieth century, and into the twenty-first. In as much as any imagined character can speak for an author, the following words from Sue Dobson, the freelance journalist from *The Nightmarkets* (1985), could well be Wearne's: 'Take any normal street of average length ... / Simply concentrate on / a street of a suburb: *that's* mindblowing!'[2]

Wearne's scrupulous casting of individual characters from Australian social and political life is a delight. His characters are thoroughly assorted – prominent and not-so-prominent types appear and reappear across individual narratives or across bundles of narratives: schoolteachers and adolescent school students, lawyers, politicians, journalists, drug-dealers and other underworld figures, parlour hostesses, white collar criminals, church ministers and land developers. A hallmark of his inventiveness is that they are also genuinely ordinary folk who live ordinary lives – occasionally scandalous or seedy – in the terraces and backyards of Australian society. Another sorting would distinguish them as singles and friends, mums and dads, daughters and sons, and extended family. Here is the full poem 'On The Road To Gundagai':

> After church the drive, the singsong: Dad in tenor mode
> winds the Vauxhall down Mount Dandenong Road;
>
> lulled, Mum's glad, these patterns still keep:
> Janet reading, Carol pulling faces, Margie asleep.
>
> Till, beyond such certainties, each arrives
> (stride-, stroll- or stumbling through their lives)
>
> out of those soul-on-sleeve
> days, with what was/ is/ might be something to believe.

> So Dad dies, Mum re-marries and shifts,
> Janet lectures, Carol designs, Margie drifts.
>
> Oh millstone/ loadstar
> (that time of faiths/ a Sunday in the car)
>
> behold your future, its, by extension, splendour:
> welcome, ladies to The Age of Gender![3]

This melodic vignette poses a willowy sketch of characters — Dad, Mum and three daughters — about whom we know nothing apart from the narrator's slice-of-life anecdotes, set to the rhythm of a well-known Australian popular song from the early 1920s (it might be the song the Dad is singing). Those characters keep the narrative afloat, propelling the shifts between an historical note and a lyrical note, which break into each other through the melancholy wit and irony of the narrator. And the narrative itself? It is a yarn about the banality and pure serendipity of time, told within the time experience of memory. If Wearne's poetry takes a measure of social particularities from the past, as many reviewers have pointed out, it is nearly always with a view to how they sound for a contemporary present. He finds in the past something meaningful that can be imaginatively reconstructed as continuous with a modern equivalence, a dialogue that looks in two directions at people and culture in time.

In Wearne's monologues and narratives, plot often plays a subsidiary role to his characters. He ruminated in a recent interview:

> As for narrative techniques, in writing *The Nightmarkets* I recall adopting the motto 'Take care of the characters and the plot will take care of itself.' Well it probably did — if you could call what resulted a plot, for really, I didn't know the book had one. In *The Lovemakers*, 'events commenced, to improve', though I doubt if these could be summarised as an overall 'plot'. One overall narrative then? No. Overall narratives? Yes.[4]

The Nightmarkets runs to 10,750 lines, its ten monologues cover a year in the lives of its six characters. One distinct narrative thread is politics: two of the characters are running for political office and references to political events and topics filter through the narrative — the Vietnam War and conscription protests of the 1960s, ASIO, Communism, the dismissal of 1975, to name a few. Yet politics, notwithstanding its significance, is largely ancillary to the everyday observations and introspections in each character's monologue. One reviewer described *The Nightmarkets* as a contingent narrative:

> ... the primary involvement is with what each monologue
> implies of a particular life. We are drawn not so much into the
> momentum of a story as into a whole existence, a personal web
> of connections which — inevitably, but almost as if incidentally —
> involves the progression of events.[5]

This could be said of *The Lovemakers* too. Comprising two long books —
Book One, Saying all the great sexy things (2001) and *Book Two, Money and
nothing* (2004) — *The Lovemakers* has multiple narrative strands and numerous
characters, and it experiments profusely with poetic forms.

Wearne leans on plot in his monologues and narratives only in so far as
it illuminates how his characters or narrators speak, and especially how their
language persistently shifts and circles. Their thoughts turn on things they are
involved in, whether on a dilemma or on events that are part of ordinary (even
extraordinary) goings-on. We are drawn into layers of their consciousness
while they talk to someone: a reader, someone in their group, some outsider, or
themselves. Once in a while, the poet himself is one of the created characters.
In this selection, a lively interplay is set up between narrator and poet in
'Operation Hendrickson', an unconventional twenty-poem narrative sequence.
The narrator Robert Hendrickson recalls anecdotes from his school days in the
early 1960s, which includes bringing his old school-mate Alan Wearne into
the narrative and, ironically, asking the poet to tell his story: 'Wearney you
needn't believe because / he's just making it up for *Proper Gander*, / his rag.
'Hey Wearney, write my memoirs / then put them into your *Proper Gander*'.[6]
The sequence plays subtly with the doubleness of the two authorial roles,
masterfully rendering tough stories and school reminiscence with pathos and
humour.

Wearne's specific interest in his characters is in their inner life, their
attitudes, biases, beliefs, and in human behaviour: the moment-to-moment
intimacies and exchanges of daily suburban and urban experience. In an
interview, he acknowledged, 'It can be said that I have obsessions rather than
ideas, these obsessions dominated by particular people or groups, often based
on folk I've met, known or (like Terry Clark) read about'.[7] His folk are a broad
species of women and men who belong with their particular social group or
groups by virtue of birth, economic chance or choice. In the short narrative
'Neutral Bay', for example, the speaker is a female courier for the Mr Asia Drug
Syndicate. She meditates the ordinary ease of it — 'I'd get in from the airport
after midnight / and wait a day, till someone came around, / unloaded me and

made me *Thanks sweetheart* / $15,000 richer' – then a restlessness:

> What did I think I was,
> not old enough to break the law? What law?
> By then the only law I had to keep
> was getting away with knowing Terry Clark,
> so yes I was old enough. I did it,
> did it often enough; and whoever I was
> I just needed an identity, even if
> I didn't need an identity. I was smart and
> waiting about on the fringes of Terry Clark's
> banal life, hardly knew what I did,
> except that I was that damn special.

And finally an unexpected poignancy where the female speaker admits peril, with a brief semblance of self-compassion and contrition:

> Giving myself a week away from spending
> I caught a light aircraft back to the folks,
> stayed up to near midnight
> doing gossip with Mum. Of course
> someone's kid was 'into drugs',
> always someone's kid and always drugs.
>   And I thought
> *Who knows what The Organisation's doing*
> *right now: cutting, grinding and packing;*
> *delivering, collecting and waiting*
> and how I never wanted to feel damn special again.
> But *Thanks a lot sweetheart* of course I did.[8]

If there is something to be drawn out of Wearne's word 'obsessions', it is in his turning over of the suppressed itches and compulsions of his characters.

When *Saying all the great sexy things* was published in 2001, Wearne was quoted as saying it 'is about love'.[9] We might add sex and friendship. *Money and nothing* continues those narratives and also broadens to the entrepreneurial excess of the 1980s, and a tranche of criminal personalities. Kevin Joy, head of the Joy Boys Drug Syndicate and a central character in that second volume, repeatedly mingles criminality and love in his long dramatic monologue 'Nothing but Thunder':

Don't I know what the world needs now, Mister Bacharach!
People want and I'm their kind of Cupid ...
love first and profit only later, I tell you
that makes for real danger. And they're frightened.[10]

Love, sex and friendship and the more public catalysts of money and power, are prominent motivators for human behaviour throughout Wearne's work. A question to ask about them is: what distinction is made here between public affairs and private activity? Very likely none at all, in the sense that his public and private squares are equivalently ordinary. This poetry can make the ordinary seem absurd or comical, and it can turn sharply to satire or to amusement, and just as delicately to poignancy. It gives us the interesting ordinariness of people in public life as not very different from the interesting ordinariness of people in their private lives.

Wearne reflected in a 2011 interview on the importance of 'the everyday or my imaginings of an everyday':

> ... the very concept of writing about such things is a superb challenge. Can one truly make poetry out of such material without banality? Past examples give me confidence that it can be done.[11]

Foremost amongst his influences are those poets who observe the low dramas (and melodramas) of ordinary social and political mores, re-treading vernacular registers in tying language poetically to the everyday. In an interview, he names a significant predecessor from the fourteenth century: 'What guided me? Since at least my teens I've worked for an outfit called *Narrative Verse in English*, whose founder was a man called Geoff, Geoff Chaucer'. He adds a number of other precursors in long narrative poetry – Pope, Byron, Frost, Kenneth Koch[12] – and especially singles out a trio of mid-Victorian masters of narrative verse, monologues and dramatic monologues: 'Clough, Meredith and Browning more or less challenged me: 'We can do it ... go on ... can you?"'.[13]

Each monologue and narrative in this selection has its own fidelity to the ordinary, not least in matters of love. 'Roger, or Of Love and its Anger' from *The Lovemakers* is a superb sequence of twenty-six experimental rhymed sonnets. Roger's voice shifts back and forth between extremity and composure as he speaks to his psychiatrist about his wife's infidelity. Here is all of Sonnet 18 'Grit (ii)'; 'Wonderboy' is his diminutive for his wife's lover:

It won't square with ladies, but getting decked
is a compliment; if you can hit and be hit
so can he. When fighting implies a certain respect
why thump your loathed one? (It's better to spit.)
Wonderboy deserved neither. If hardly innocent
his acts were love-fuelled.

       As if direct from the shit
of battle I wished I could've signalled this opponent
You and Barb ... d'd'dit dardardar d'd'dit ...
don't send reinforcements just rest my fears
and tell me why.

       So exit thoughts of 'Put up y'dooks.'
Today's far more a case of this: combs raised and fighting fit
two more Chanticleers
strut respective barnyards (mine, Wonderchook's)
pecking into their wondergrit.[14]

This sonnet is Roger's implicit version of the marriage. Interestingly, his own proclivity as a swinger is not mentioned – it rates just a slant reference in three of the other sonnets. Here, and elsewhere through the sequence, his thought and language feel barely within his rhetorical control, while his speaking manner and his words are tethered to an apparent cool self-possession. The sequence is an homage to Meredith's 'Modern Love', and its epigraph is from Clough's 'Amours de Voyage', but it is thoroughly Browning-esque in its character moves of Roger's condescension, hostility, disdain and ultimately expedient pragmatism. Throughout these twenty-six sonnets, Wearne noticeably creates interruptions to thought by means of punctuation: brackets, italics, ellipses, colons, semicolons. In fact, interruption is a frequent habit, almost a method, in his poetry. A noticeable break or pause in a speaker's utterance, or a syntactic shift to illuminate a quick burst of sudden clarity or perhaps dense confusion, can signal intense emotions in a speaker. The result is a restlessness and suppleness of vocabulary in his work.

In Kevin Joy's long monologue 'Nothing but Thunder', Wearne experiments with the combined tension and liberality of the unmetered line. Set in a bar, Joy talks to Chrissie, an intoxicated would-be drug courier, about Sophie, his young upper middle-class lawyer and girlfriend:

Out on the tan track my head was swampy with ideas,
gelling slowly into schemes. Next time sure.
But Soph 'n' me changed gears: relaxing into parties,

wine, coke, sleep and each other.

One Saturday

she drove me to her old school fair, my tête-a-tête
with class. Class? Couldn't I buy out the lot? And spent
a second, even less, seeing my retirement. One more run say?
Imagine: wiping the frigging slate … to what?
There must be a next deal and a next. That's all.
Why join those mutts just wanting to exist? I need
to live, to feel myself curl round and into every
part of fate.[15]

What makes this dramatic monologue poetic? For this reader, it is the lineations:
in particular, the litheness of Wearne's long lines, characterising Kevin Joy as
continually poised for the (sometimes clamorous) quickenings that will propel
his narrative. Those lines modulate between moods, a change of mood turning
on a cadence. This poetry may not be consistently compact in its imagery, but it
is tight in its rhythm, echoing and re-shaping from one line to the next, while
also surprisingly varying from one to the next.

The groundnote of Wearne's vernacular is the audibility of his words
and phrases as a movement of conversational sounds and gestures. A kernel
of that narrative voice first appeared in two breakthrough poems in his first
book *Public Relations* (1972): 'Saint Bartholomew Remembers Jesus Christ as
an Athlete' (written in 1967, when he was eighteen) and 'Warburton 1910'
(written in 1972).[16] He went on to develop that voice in 'Out Here' and it has
carried forward into all corners of his subsequent work. Wearne has taken up
an idiom of conversation in verse, from utmost subtlety to a channelling of
wild and unrestrained characters who parade a lack of self-censorship.

His vernacular style can be interchangeably restless and delicate. Take
the discerning tones in 'Chatswood: Ruth Nash Speaks', a narrative about the
historical, unsolved deaths of Gib Bogle and Margaret Chandler in Sydney on
1 January 1963. In the lines below, the more graceful notes intersperse with
roughened-up ballad rhythms. Ruth's observational poise is irreverent and
witty:

… and we are, in best sellers or movies, near press-ganged to pretend
how simple, bland beginnings might prologue a ludicrous end,

So there's Gib on arrival lightfooting it down our hall,
And there's Gib a day later lightfooting bugger all.

We think we know the limits? We're merely to follow this text:
Lives unfold lives fold, here's one hour here's the next.[17]

Perhaps taking a cue from the feminist momentum of his own era, Wearne invents a plurality of women characters. Those voices often convey a sense of historical continuity with past generations in Australian social culture, and equally of projecting to the future. As I was writing this, Alan Wearne remarked in conversation that his invention of women characters comes from the fact they are fifty percent of the population.[18] It was a dry remark, with a plain truth. His imagining of the ordinariness of humanity reckons with difference in the lives of women and men, unaffectedly so. In his first verse narrative 'Out Here' (1976), five of nine monologues are from women, younger and older. Three are in the present selection: teenager Tracey Izzard, girlfriend of Brett Viney who harms himself with a knife at school; Marian Viney, Brett's mother; and Lucy Martinson, the deputy principal. In *The Nightmarkets*, three of the six main characters are women: Terri, a parlour hostess; Elise McTaggart, widow of a Liberal politician and mother of John McTaggart, head of a new political party; and Sue Dobson, whose monologue 'Climbing Up the Ladder of Love' is included here. Dobson's take on the feminist condition is a robust piece of self-creation, nicely time-located:

> We've entered the Eighties:
> it's *our* decade, what your home and schooling
> bred you for. Though the Movement may've quit even cooling
> years back, simply to freeze,
> it's time any educated woman must seize
> her inheritance to all that liberation.
> And no use bemoaning this occasion
> as transient (they all are) he can, ought to be, is your equal.
> Life's not a sequel upon sequel
> of boyfriends, their hang-ups and triumphs. Realise you're *not* twenty-three
> and some mere boy's girl. You can be me me *me*
> at last.[19]

The Nightmarkets is a classic in its social and historical particularity, and its bounty with language. Those lines are so incisive that it is easy not to notice the complex intricacy of tones. Dobson's monologue, written in rhyming couplets, is played out in a context not simply of her feminism but her profession as a journalist and her relationship with McTaggart, including her role as his biographer.

The scope of Wearne's inventiveness with characters is in finding a voice that is appropriate to each, and in registering unique experiences. In 'Anger Management: a South Coast Tale' (2017), a young mother reflects on the excitement and desire of a new relationship and how it intensifies and disintegrates, almost imperceptibly:

> He won't hit you, yet;
> just takes an arm, pushing it up your back
> to ask 'And what about what *I'm* feeling?'
> You've known him how many months
> so what are you feeling? How about
> *Sorry mate, just don't quite get it*
> or more likely *Am I to blame?*
> *Well I never deserved this!*[20]

This woman's soliloquy holds sharpness and tremor as she steps through a pathology of behaviours. It is an all-too-familiar complex of reconciliation and calm in a progression of coercions: the silent treatment, accusations, intimidation and violence. The speaker verbalises her thoughts to herself, consciously and sometimes distractedly, to get an anchor on her experience of being blindsided.

In implicit contrast to those tones is a recent monologue 'Near Believing', which reads as a dauntless satire on clerical hypocrisy and child sexual abuse. The speaker, Father John, is a married, former Anglican, now Roman Catholic priest:

> At the seaside
> whilst she and I paced the length of the strand,
> I tried explaining, not in sermon terms,
> nor talkback terms, but terms for a teenage girl
> with her over-extended crush: 'Let's stop, please.
> I'll be wedding someone else one day. Thanks for understanding.
> Hardly an hour elapses when I'm not announcing
> *Sorry if you feel I used you Toni, I understand,*
> *I used myself and my vocation.*'[21]

'Near-believing' has substantial discomforts for a reader, heightened by a disturbing frankness, the language cleaving to Father John's impiety and his trail of rebuttals and delusions as he tells his story. Wearne's more criminal personalities all seem to share a similar distorted perception of their own aberrant behaviour. He unmasks their bearings through a huge variety of moods, angles and pitch.

But the protagonist in another remarkable recent monologue, 'Waitin' for the Viet Cong' (2017), is a sceptic who is quite at home with truth. The retiree female speaker's story of a private love and a family predicament is at times agonisedly witty, and at times tender. Her tale settles on two narratives from her youth: her political activism as a university student and her disappearance one Parisian winter in pursuit of Antoinette, a French exchange student whom she met at secondary school. This monologue plays with memory and the nature of family history. The female speaker carries the narrative for what turns out to be a whole family saga – the mosaic of her reminiscence includes anecdotes and words from her late mother, her father, her sister and her sister's spouse. Her recollection of meeting Antoinette includes a smile at herself, and a memorable tune:

> This was Antoinette and I:
> some enchanted evening you may see this someone
> you'll wish to see again, again, again, then
> fly to my side and guessing I'll understand ask
> *Where exactly are you from and what exactly*
> *do they do there?*[22]

As for her politicking with fellow students, 'The Collective … my people, people ablaze / with all that kind of courage History supplies', the hope is that

> the greater stories might commence:
> all those things we'd live to see happen, happening:
> getting rid of Imperialism for starters,
> after which anything bourgeois.[23]

The speaker's tale of student rebellion and rescue become family-venerated in the words of her late mother, 'this tale she told / (eyes wide alight in their bewildered pride)'; and her father, '*She's our rebel and nobody else's*';[24] and her sister and her sister's spouse, 'You realise … it was their networks found you …'. Or, as the speaker says, 'History, / unalterable History'. This ageing woman's own lightly ironic voice recaptures the dogmas and paraphernalia of a spirited younger self with wry joy, but only her revolutionary zeal becomes part of family lore: 'I put aside telling Mother of 'Antoinette the Sequel' / but then she died. Dad remarried so I told them, / humanism all the way.'[25] That last assertion might be referable, with a degree of irony, to something like this:

We knew Struggle, we knew Truth,
  Knew Hué and Hai Phong,
Served such causes in our youth,
  Waitin' for the Viet Cong.
Whilst Johnson, Nixon strafed the North,
Bellowed each July the Fourth:
"Longin' for the Viet Cong to win girls,
  Screamin' for the Viet Cong!"[26]

That ballad, in six stanzas, is quoted (invented? remembered?) to conclude the monologue.

On a similar edge, some lines from Sue Dobson (and maybe even the poet), written much earlier:

For this most fascinating thing in the world

addicts me: women and men. All the skirmishes, battles,

truces, treaties, all the incongruous attrition

of civil war and reconstruction, as,

between flare-ups, we resume some spongey armistice.[27]

There is a strange largesse in that catalogue of part-failures. But largesse in many directions comes naturally to Alan Wearne as a prime mark of all his poetry. We hope that this selection is a surprise and pleasure to read right through, in whatever order a reader's curiosity may take.

Michelle Borzi

Michelle Borzi is a critical reviewer and essayist specialising in poetry. Awarded a PhD on W.H. Auden's poetry in 2003 by the University of Melbourne, her writings on Australian poetry over the last two decades are widely published. Based in Melbourne, her work as a freelance researcher includes editing poetry manuscripts and sessional teaching of poetry and poetics.

Endnotes

1. Alan Wearne and Michael Brennan, 'Interview with Alan Wearne', *Poetry International*, 1 July 2011, https://www.poetryinternational.org/pi/cou_article/19026/Interview-with-Alan-Wearne

2. Alan Wearne, *The Nightmarkets.* (Ringwood: Penguin Books Australia Ltd, 1985) 64.

3. Alan Wearne, *Near Believing: Selected Monologues and Narratives 1967-2021.* (Waratah: Puncher and Wattmann, 2022) 135.

4. Alan Wearne, 'Interview with Alan Wearne'. *The Verse Novel: Australia & New Zealand.* ed. Linda Weste. (North Melbourne: Australian Scholarly Publishing Pty Ltd, 2021) 270.

5. John Leonard, 'The Nightmarkets: Nothing Fated or Rarefied,' *Scripsi.* 4.3 (April 1987): 120.

6. Wearne, *Near Believing* 197.

7. Wearne, *The Verse Novel* 263.

8. Wearne, *Near Believing* 158.

9. Angela Bennie, 'Lawson of the suburbs finds poetry in ordinary lives,' *Sydney Morning Herald* 28 May 2002: 3.

10. Wearne, *Near Believing* 119-20.

11. Wearne and Brennan, *Poetry International Rotterdam.*

12. Wearne, *The Verse Novel* 271.

13. Wearne, *The Verse Novel* 273.

14. Wearne, *Near Believing* 94.

15. Wearne, *Near Believing* 121.

16. Alan Wearne and Michelle Borzi, 'Conversation with the author', 13 June, 2019.

17. Wearne, *Near Believing* 149.

18. Alan Wearne and Michelle Borzi. 'Conversation with the author', 18 January, 2021.

19. Wearne, *Near Believing* 64-65.

20. Wearne, Near Believing 183.

21. Wearne, *Near Believing* 226-227.

22. Wearne, *Near Believing* 188.

23. Wearne, *Near Believing* 187.

24. Wearne, *Near Believing* 186.

25. Wearne, *Near Believing* 192.

26. Wearne, *Near Believing* 193.

27. Wearne, *The Nightmarkets* 55.

from *Poems 1967-1974*

Saint Bartholomew Remembers Jesus Christ as an Athlete

Always in training. Yet helping with his work
was partly boring, sometimes even nasty.
Still, even when I felt he'd gone too far,
think *Here we go again* out came the logic
smooth as a circle, Roman-disciplined.
Brilliant. Yes. Yet never near to God.

Only when he ran.
Only when I saw him striding.
(He'd leap and throw his arms above his head.)
It really was a case of *Run with me.*
I did. And often we came down the mountains
(jogging loosely, never with a cramp)
my running partner, heading for Jerusalem,
appeared as if his feet were next to God.

This too was a feat: running for a month
(as rumour had it).
                        Sprinting in the temple
was nothing less than perfect. Tables knocked,
whips raised and money lost.
He charged them twice.

Of course revenge was needed, and his arms
were raised once more; his feet however, broken;
sort of enforced retirement. Still,
he made a comeback to end all comebacks.
                                            Once
there were ten, and I half-walking, pacing
(my room-mates, seated, limbered-up in prayer).
We stopped the noise and movement; standing still,
I heard the footsteps pounding up the stairs.

St Kilda

for Alan Wayman

Boots in a flat and flakes of orange paint,
warm lager and a friend that slit his hand.
February midnight the mercury broiled ninety,
whilst Brookes and boy-friend made it in the sand.

All drink was Abbots and I drank it, then,
back to the back of the block, rather castle-
shaped, on a lied-lease; candles, no carpet, but
at twenty a week: gas, water, a dunny; only hassle
was paying for it (or yourself, new master which
slashed the back of a hand that snatched
at this dumb and roly-poly nice nineteener, you used
for eighteen months). Soon I matched
such clowning when *Making It for March* was interrupted:
in a distressed minute I took the front-door key,
whose owner laughed, chased; I chucked it back,
as hapless residents staring down Dalgety
waited a brawl twixt two loons: wild-eye
dasher, half-dressed groover. Naught occurred.
Why? Concerns were interruptions, joking, more
with a pun than viciousness, take my word;
'cause if idiot up-tight dames might shuttle you,
day patient bin-wards, we'd whisper 'Tut, that's rough.'
And bless you a quiet hometown-even, fucking,
I hope with those boots (large, impractical) off!

Almost experience! Even I supposed, joined:
in April sick of proxying an excuse,
skolled one third Johnnie Walker neat, another
night of use and making use for use.

Warburton 1910

Sarah...of us in our chaise the photograph
shows Colin and I turning a bend towards The Ferns;
will send it soon. Introduced, fussed-over, we still laugh
as 'newlyweds'. The other guests -one's a baronet- take turns
as mama and papa: 'You babes so young...' (Often
it felt unlikely I was married.) After luncheon Mr McCracken took
us out in the motor. 'Where to Mrs?' he asked. When
that made feelings quite important this 'high toned lady' (me) looked
out over the mountains: miles of fern-gully, waterfall,
and 'To the prettiest place you know!' I replied.
If raining we never read, but pretend it's a log-cabin, all-
for-us.
            Yet, from the verandah, we saw this stupid boy who shied
a bird from a tree. I slipped hand into my husband's, watching
the willful child tread the damp lawn, slingshot aimed and smiling.

Eating Out

for Robin Rattray-Wood

Gentle, inaffluent,
susceptible to portions of pity though
a mild cynicism increased
as he left high school and
The High School Student's Union
(articulates in berets with
little yellow stars: 'Semantics, man...'
'Aww that's a cop-out, man...)
susceptible to cool, correct sympathy
(slight commitment)
any girl concerned to teach him
wines, driving, boredom.

And Nicol, she was joining NIDA yet
they kept company for a few weeks
of a dry summer (shifts and
blouses flapping over the line).
What's she like to live with?
Ahh that's romance, attainable
as clap. All construction:
a partner in sorrow would be
wonderful: poor pet, poor pet. (Such
prey we are to prey!)

Windows of dwarfs, in Xmas
the city was presentiments, expenditure,
recalling for him an earlier attempt
(each day begins a year)
'How often should I see you?'
and the mother with hands smeared
in drycleaning fluid. Nice
nice nice nice. He shivered
for their kingdom of constraint,
but no quibbles, virginity is
amazing, beautiful as the back
of Sarah's waist,

how neat it was!

       'See a show?'
                'You're hosting!'
                       Then let's.
Mrs Salmons (was it Salmons?) suspected
at least casinos: 'Where will tea
be?' Hinting at liquor, 'Eh?'
       Why it's toast, Ma'm, it's an evangelical
coffee house, Ma'm. Shook hands.
       Coming back her father beaming *Young Ones!*
and Sarah asked 'Excuse me?'
left for sleep. That body:
small, neat, redoubtable, it
seemed unfair; but quit the thought.
We were a debacle!

       This year, Nicol. On weekends,
before her course,
they trotted round the palm tree parks,
up to rotundas, her home at hand
through lime-white colonnades, there,
a lot for him:
table manners, the correct liquor. Some
minor heiress in a cheesecloth blouse
sustaining his dictum:
'My word, Marxism is exotic!'

       For last year (as a friend referred)
Les Chinois stoic in Bakeries, their cache
of humourless invective; yet oh the design!

       Living is divergence, plus
'how swell'. A trainee life-assessor and
Sarah would be very very happy. Not hers
some fuming dialectician
(their High School Student's Union pronouncing
such ministry 'Lethal as a nail gun').
Some years further
here's he, sitting in a bandstand,

the NIDA trainee saying 'Sometimes
I can't conceive of letting a man near,
you understand?'
                    Romance is, you know,
danger; though a few nights
before her parents drove Nicki
over to the flight she took him
eating. ('Daddy's a solicitor
with conscience.') Workingmen mean
a lot and the waiter asked him, him
regards wine, 'Sir?'

        Damn brief, ought to have been
forgettable (I'm forgettable too) kissing
this forthcoming actress, oh poised for
an unsorrowing wave off the tarmac:
the outsized sunglasses, the smart,
pudding-basin bum, cheesecloth.

        A lift? Please.
On his prize bush, aphis. Nicol's father
stated aphis and how to end it
(talking of steps to Mr Potter, gardener).
Yes, a lift...*with music to town*
and you in my arms...easy, adult, radio
smarmed away its 'Happy day happy day.'

from *Out Here*

Yes? 'Just...'

Lucy Martinson, deputy principal of a high school in an affluent area

I viewed the eddies of the Viney maelstrom.

Into such comfort, so well-meaning
an area, the somewhat tragedy of
a youth slashing himself.
Glancing up at my door, I viewed
him, seventeen say, hand
over his stomach as a big hero,
and I, pen held on
a sheet of school-crested paper,
gazed solemn (bit part
in a film adaptation, from set texts).
Gazed...well? Yes? 'Just...'
So he moved the hand across, lifted
and was bleeding.

Some small crisis; at once
with bandages, the ambulance completed,
I rang adults: Brett's mother and father, home
and, as they say, ranting.

(Brett, brat?) Who'd collect him?
'He'll be there a few days...' added
to settle nothing at all.
His mother took time to comprehend till
those frantic shouts, accusations,
to someone, Russell. A slow silence,
my role as teacher (oh guide!)
lost then. And was it embarrassment,
admittance to so much caricature
that untranslatable language:
the marriage brawl:
the raging, and I listened to
the woman's slow taut sighs, and yes
she would go to the District Hospital.

Oh, it's such a well-meaning area!
Yes indeed, must sparkle Sunday morning,
though I've never been over here, then,
aping what's left from fashionable stores,
after the wafer and the wine.
Why this picture, quite a snapshot,
really absurd? Women in smooth styles,
(refined, competitive) men, perhaps in
better office suits, chat after services.
Those Vineys? Could have attended I suppose;
all one has to do ask and observe.
Yet now they've gone
it seems a week, months though,
that Brett slashed, her husband left
and she that smooth-styled red-eyed
mother marked time. Will she set out
finding a further father for Brett
and the others? A daughter, here, fourteen,
had to attend to her; the girlfriend
first, second the friend, then
we discover Sharyn the sister. Priorities!

But a father, as I said, a husband? Doubt it.
Pleasant to be unmarried,
take my Aunt, quasi-bohemian, ached
for a salon. ('But where were the artistes, Lucy?')
Aunt loved her situation, relished this one.
'Fine Lucy fine, show the rascal certain things
he'll want...' Brett, Aunty? She doesn't hear,
I return to my desk, homework.

Try (it's said, am told) one may be
participates, as I rang into that argument:
lumps of pity, justification, abuse;
those shrill over-the-phone accents;
that slash, one B.R. Viney slicing himself
on the stomach, down at the dunnies,
as the siren started classes.
Aunt slaps down such events
into precepts. 'Nonsense Lucy,

you did all you had to, could.'
Did so, no emotional wet nurse
to some adolescent
I didn't know existed.
'An unsettling, Lucy, and
for any sake don't turn it into pity!'

Where, Aunt, do you think they live?
Gracious, ivied, wrought-iron terraces
aren't in *that* well-meaning garden-land,
with some Russell husband.
Aunt, that area hasn't community
hasn't responsibility:
who won't serve but want to
be served; joint names, sighs and raves
and a child (family term)
comes into my office.

Oh, and the boss says:
'The Vineys seem rather inward,
canteen, working-bees, committees
aren't their territory,
save one unofficial dinner-dance.
They've caused no trouble though,
you're the first contact really.'
Yes. 'Also,' says Mr McNamara,
'Viney seemed attached to
young Tracey Izzard. Tell her?
Before rumours, it would be best,
you know how women, well,
know.' Said I would.
'Okay,' says Mac, 'and
perhaps Simon Egan, Viney's, well best friend,
more sense than well his mate,
you understand?' He offered me
boiled lollies from a jar.
I took a fistful, left,
sent for the children.

And if I was shaking, yes,
what of the later day his father came
justifying all but this terrible disturbance.
'My wife has gone to her father's' he added.
And, 'His bringing-up, where, where
in his bringing-up?' Brought-up Mr Viney,
oh how was the pup trained?
Is Mr Viney 'honest'? Haven't
any idea, nouse, care on the gentleman,
his deals and dealings, though
this family bears makings of Viney,
the blood etc which we drained up
with rinser attached slop-bucket
and raggy mop. *Blood*, stupid term
for there's the divorce, or something.
They seem, around my age, maybe
their courtship, my degree (honours) course,
kept in time, in time to Master of something,
my next (nth) course, their divorce.
Find it uncanny and 'courtship' such
an applicable fifties term.

I was new there, he
never was my student and gone now
as the unimportant piece of
my life, he almost was
(was coincidence…) Yet let's not
consider that appointments, transfers,
births, simple attractions have sent
Brett Viney and I creeping toward
each other's life, I helping,
he no, let's not consider.
For then he left, they left,
the house was sold to anything.
Tenderness, I know is an over-used
noun, so I couldn't care
whatever housed those blunt,
brawling elder Vineys,
deserved anything. Though *tenderness*?
It's wrong to send three children out

-not as some boo-hoo orphan saga,
rather because they're people
with parents, and one had
the stupid courage to try being
a person with parents.
-Come here, look I'm showing,
showing you, I can hate
better than either you who
only loathe each other.
Does this 'mere boy' so dominate
me, now that I did what I had to?
Unlikely. Still he steps into the door-way,
that hand, stoic over the wound,
as if to claim this well-meaning
area and school, in benediction: 'Just…'

Inventory. One, I viewed, two
don't often, three, never I hope again:
glimpsing the eddy, this
malformation, scandal, basis,
his mode of protest and relief.
'But why Brett (isn't it?) why?'
Oh his shrug and *oh just, just*
mucking around with a knife.

Home

Marian Viney, a mother, wife, and part-time market researcher

One's heard of women out here
in my class, income receiving bracket,
trotting around to some slim, smooth,
blanky bland agent, to rent a house.
The Stayfresh breath, the 'May-I-help-you?'
phone noises, smoothing aside those
inconveniences of your first home away
from Russell, children, from your
old man and name. Oh well...
I've work, pocket money and,
where we can begin, homes,
each Monday, Wednesday, Thursday afternoon
for holiday plans, brands preferred,
parties supported, opinions sustained.
And all my girlfriends, as it were, give over,
chat at tea. I'm 'brisk' and told so
(not every woman is, I keep to myself).
Yet my father has ensured, rightly,
how some of his daughters are 'brisk'.

Yes Lorraine, that raver,
all her woolly, misplaced philanthropy,
acts like an heiress in say Harlem
Naples or Calcutta. That's not correct,
she's what, thirty, and I *ought* to,
ought to visit the clinic, I know
she's doing a great damn job, it just upsets
her preaching, her arguments with father,
Russ and the nation. Our sisters
are pygmies to you, pet;
if only you weren't so stubbornly, defiantly
righteous! Or couldn't be. Look, look
at the miles I clock, the dull *don't knows*,
some rudeness which one must treat
tenderly, coy, my sweet nature, truce,
a masquerade from home, from Russell.

And given imagination once: the flirtings,
the pipe, the hair styled 'chunky', squash,
I thought, of course
the Hugh Hefner of Karinya Crescent; god,
my husband's irredeemable!
Oh yet, I cannot remember correctly (nine years,
eight years back?) but, when mother died,
there was a punctuation in my life, ours, paused,
established itself; had thought of
snapping, thought of anything:
his women – out of season shooting trips –
visits to the brother he conned
time over time (the Viney name!).
Women! When it has happened, I'm sorry
for that poor little squirrel who, as it occurred,
knew him as 'Ben O'Keefe'. Russ,
when he prefers, has humour, grimy humour.

I had thought to leave, though it was
too grand then, that I, some house and home;
but we held, it sufficed. He had the sympathy
I needed. And Mother, my Mouse-mother,
plaything of that passionate rampage
A. A. McNab, shifted away eight nine (ten?)
years ago, and, I assume saved
what we've decided to finish.

And should *I* continue? indeed. This girl's something,
and though Lorraine knows I work
she suspects me. I held to Russ,
had kids not opinions, no mouse Ma'm,
mind, but to be daughter, sister and wife
to three remarkable maniacs, plus mother
to some fool with an Army Disposal Store knife...
O Brett, son, we were, are crazy for
playthings and pocket money, but
your father and I, until recently, held,
we tried. Try and care Brett. Care.

So, to my son's Tracey:
she has a long pale neck, slight ginger hair
and this unnerving abundance, poise.
One almost wishes flaws...okay,
freckles are sprayed, patching
around her throat, her face.
She's tall and her hair cropped
almost viciously; seventeen
and knows how to wear jewellery.
Came round, today in fact, began talks
as it were, since Brett's event and
Russell left. It's not as if she sits
'Uh-huh uh-huh', to all I throw,
she likes Russ, is sceptical still.
And I? Lorraine with all her slum-
acquired wisdom might snap
'Jealousy' (leaving it at that).
Tracey is poise, asks and admits,
strange that I, the brisk
almost career woman, should bother,
be unsettled so by Tracey
one red-haired fifth-former my son
might love might care for, but couldn't
dream of letting into our Viney brawls.
Care for small things Tracey,
for often it was fine just fine.
Yes there were women,
but he cared for me and gave...
none of the moles he, well, obtained,
lasted any amount. It's Bohemians
have these long-time love-affairs, not us.
Lorraine would know, shared her bed
with half the...no, I'm incorrect
prejudging; the only time they met,
she got on well with Tracey, she
knows her, probably better than I
know Tracey, or Lorraine. It never fits.

I won't prejudge. Even on marriages
(forbid it!) little business.
Yet I was green. Not in you know, well,
the idea, being brought up on homes
and families. When Dad came back
(the Middle East Campaign over)
something was established.
I enthralled that five had so much
meaning, (Lorraine to be born and
Marl a bubba). Yet, how could I say,
it meant something positive; into that,
that spirit, some years later I married;
now I must find meaning again or,
should I say regain a positive, brisk poise.
Words words, they didn't defeat us,
gradually I wanted meaning, something
(pocket money?). Darling, you wished
for the spring or summer bride, perpetual…
but no I won't judge Russ,
yes please, some luck and forgiveness.

Just recall *our I don't wanna go
to the party with you/ I don't wanna go
to the dance?* Remember, and we met
through friends (we haven't seen since
one wet holiday, could have moved).
It seems quite natural, yet queer,
that chance could have us
living together, so long so long.
Now we've continued something,
not so different; just sealing the 'living'.
We'll meet, often I assume,
you never hit and I'm
no half-way candidate for activists
to gloat upon. There's our children, yes,
seem relatively sane. My job of course:
the kids, not so you can pick-up
and bed anything under thirty,
(if they want it!) but the kids,
mine honey, imagine *you* trying

(granted trying), to bring up
Sharyn now, or Danny. Throughout my
shall I say career, you, you,
always preferred a mother. Now,
you've one. Honey, am not bitter,
we can, after some settlement, talk
on something: kids work friends family,
(all we have) am sorry that this,
our experiment I suppose, oh gone
gone gone. Such sorting out we've
engaged on now, isn't fun,
but discipline I'd say, as father would,
and harmless. Harmless darling, like,
remember our corny, oh perfect
ship-of-life wedding and reception?

Oh Dad, if you feel cheated, say if
the plans for something fell, don't.
It is our what, time, (Lorraine says 'class')
something. 'Class!' Lorraine don't
moralize, you're closeted in alley-ways
and slums...I'm sorry, wrong. Eight years
older with kids and a kitchen, I understand *your* life;
still, whatever this 'liberation' is, pet, sister,
how about out here, out here.
You'd say I'd acquiesced Lorraine, no,
though I still say to that mistake, bastard Russell:
'Yes, you nor I understood, please understand,
leave me darling, but recall: *I just
wanna stay here and love you* remember it?
Yes, still glad I know you.'

Growing

Tracey Izzard, Brett's girlfriend, a high school student

There's someone's homing pigeons
flanking above the last roost
they'll have over the area,
the broad triangle
(a loose high school pennant)
a wing abandoned and tossed to
turn and return. He can't come back,
though, what, three railway stations down
is all the distance. Yes there were
people, plentiful and concerned and,
although he was Brett, my Brett,
I didn't have to answer anything;
rather they suggested 'Go home…'
Miss Martinson called Simon and I
from classes, whilst at recess he
took me to the gate, no Brett but
someone, an arm over my shoulder,
big lumpy Simon Egan:
'They'll leave the area,' calling it
'the Viney gloom. 'Likely', I said,
and felt like closing my eyes.
Hadn't felt like thrashing-out
in a fit, yet Simon said
(reassuring, almost Simon demands)
'Brett, he will get better.' Thank you.
I looked up and left him.
We knew as much, that the stupid
stupid marriage treated Brett
and the others in convenience.
Though they were nice people,
Dad thought them funny,
whilst Mother stayed silent.
Yet anyhow, that's the tragedy I guess,
they shrugged between arguments
and then the children, only then Brett.
We've had to learn this year.

(Some girlfriends having mastered
Shorthand-and-typing simply
continue, let it all occur.) Oh yes
the 1848 revolution. To be honest
Brett didn't want me to do it
said he'd done Modern History,
found it difficult.
Brett's brainy, though he worries
and doesn't work. What he's done
is cancel out this year; I'm *not
to worry*. Been repeating that phrase
over *not to worry, not to...*
unconvincing. Didn't *act*
as I was stabbed, but took a
week or so from school; maybe
my mother wouldn't speak, she
didn't care for Brett, maybe
I watched too many mid-day movies,
great old stars counselling 'Pull yourself
together girl!' So I got up,
one muggy humid morning,
depressing day, and thought,
'When they see me, they won't understand,
pregnancy rumours I suppose
have flung my name and Brett's
around the school. Looks as obvious.'
Well I can trust Marcia, Annabelle, maybe
Jenny and Simon of course, enough.
There's Legal Studies to catch up,
Modern History, Geography. It wasn't
a case of *pull yourself together,
up and out of it*. I love him,
always shall Brett, however to
let him dominate me so, and
his parents, there's no issue, Tracey,
would they bother your account?
Did Brett bother you, his father-and mother's snapping
sniping? They seemed so 'Having
a gay-and-hearty.' Remember

when they went out dining,
allowing Brett, I and others, to play records,
good that night, amazing, well,
they came in the door at twelve-fifteen,
looking just like a partnership;
taking his coat off, the vest gave
the appearance of some gambler, she
was in velvet, my parents would be tatty,
never yelling 'Gay-and-hearty!'

'Sometimes, these rows,' oh yes
sometimes he told me, Brett did,
just in passing, Lorraine of course
sought to tell all, trying to pass
the blame nowhere. No *Aunt* Lorraine,
that was evident, she came round,
argued politics with Mr Viney,
'I don't aim to be right Russell, I am!'
Her sister's posture, he slamming the wire door
left the kitchen, Mrs Viney trotting after,
it seemed the only time he gave way, habits
collapsed, had him muttering in the garden.
'Trace,' said Lorraine, familiar, 'Don't don't
get involved with any Viney.' An order?
a threat? There's Brett. And I still like
'Gay-and-Hearty.' That he should leave
a family, let alone a room, slamming,
it doesn't square. Other girls...?
But Mrs V was so nice, organised
excellent, withheld, yes and posture
straight back and unlike her sister
didn't ask to call her name.
She has to be Mrs anything. Viney, Egan.

The pigeons again!
Fly away Peter, fly away Brett,
come back darling, even to call you that,
oh I could be drunk again,
do I, did I, really love him?

Kept so much away. 'Gracious!' Mother said.
'Some strange boy you had.'
'Leave her,' Dad replied. Upset. I was.

So I suppose I love him,
Simon, I, and others knew, something,
fouled our friend. Oh he always
respected me and didn't need reminding
of well, you know, things. He's neat,
not horribly though, didn't go out much,
except parties, like.
We'd much to talk about, not like some
girls do, how they'll get married,
naming the kids Jason and Melissa,
where they'll live. How much rubbish!
No, Brett would give me books to read
and Dad would say 'At last,
something other than fan magazines.' And I,
'Oh Dad – dy' (playing it up)
'I'm far too old for *Dolly*!'
And he'd be chirpy, whenever Brett arrived
(except at Mother's migraine times)
and he'd delight for a while in 'Mr Izzard...'
till, 'The name's Paul, Brett, remember,
though the wife is still, you understand...'

You know what I like, liked the best
apart from being with Brett, you know?
Dad's greenhouse, Saturday Morning.
Where we've talked about Brett
and Mum, her delicate problems.
He's not like a father then, an adult,
grown-up, as which he treats me;
love it, the mist outside in late autumn,
it's nine o'clock, the radio has finished with
Mr Jack Plumridge, For the Home Gardener.
And here's one,
love the stink of Blood-and Bone,
something is going-on, you know,

growing as Dad says. Not, he adds
like the area. Your mother and I
came when this was land not
houses, stupid to tear up space,
thought we were pioneering, only
to have them come, move in move out,
after us. To blame as any.

Where were the cow-pats, pathways,
blackberries, pigeon roosts (one left)?
If it were by a log fire, camping,
or in a hall half filled with cranks
I'd be chilled, feel creepy, yet it's here
with shrubs and plants and
good old Blood-and Bone, that I
accept, things growing, him raving,
fog and the suburb out there.
And Brett? Leaving but spaces Dad,
would mean no Brett, no school,
and, if someone had your plans before,
no you nor mum nor I nor any greenhouse.

Growth, I suppose, having the plants burst
slowly under glass under (those mornings)
fog; even pigeons trying to locate
something apart from the roofs
attending their old last home.
Growing I cannot fully say it, but
even Brett, ashamed as he could be,
gone down the line, maybe ever,
he's sorting things out. Maybe I
wasn't much in the reckonings,
all I can hear are rumours,
but all I believe are plants moving,
birds re-turning. (The rest, him,
his books, our talks,
arms over my shoulder,
that 'Gay-and-hearty',
maybe spaces, windy spaces).

Like it's some ghost town

Brett Viney, Russell and Marian's eldest child, a high school student

There was a corridor,
everyone turned keys
at locker lines, locker times.
Sometimes though, lunches would
be left lying overnight
and a few rats, just might,
trickle across the drain, grounds
into our school,
it wasn't nice, though
one became excited
exulted maybe, as at
a carnival, cries cries
would commence (near windows).
It pestered women,
made shrieking some
momentary pastime as
a troop of searching rodents
padded their progress
over the asphalt. Yet,
wo don't you know
nothing continues, the scraps
cleared with Mr McNamara's
Operation Spring Clean,
the women shrieked at *us*,
lumpy Casanovas, but finally
a fourth form bird
murmured quietly: 'Another mouse.'

She was Tracey, staying away
from the Interschool Swimming Sports,
that grand goulash of mock-rivalry,
pennants and streamers, orders,
school monstrously mock, at least
at home you knew it earnest enough.
Yet I digress. She was Tracey, won't be my wife

now or ever? Come off it!
Dreams-kiddie-wishes. Tracey!

In the yard an hour after school,
she and I would pace it, hand
(at last) in hand,
like it's some ghost town. Really,
I loved it the best, an extra
anyone, would have been conflict.
almost a family. Sharyn caught up
to us, once, 'Been muckin' around,
what y'think?' She's a tart,
I think, but it's her life as
mine is. Everyone's having dinner
shortly, all day seems centred on
the meal; Dad used to be up there
either laughing or not laughing, seems
to enjoy a hot meal, carving it,
pouring over the gravy, such,
is going on in thousands of homes,
and it's all right for Bornstein to yell:
'Conformist!' but he eats, all eat,
and he's never stabbed, knives aren't
for one use, take this,
bought it at Carneys, Elizabeth St.
Really *that* wasn't stupid, I mean
there's thousands around, it could be
an ornament, but these scars here,
Christ I was game, took courage;
Simon admires my scars and courage
wouldn't say so though, too solemn,
head full of Mendelssohn, Handel,
and it's surprising how much he knew,
not only suspected of us:
me, and Father, Mother, Tracey.

Tracey and I tussled
beside a lemon tree, hardly beautiful,
ourselves in the too warm October

evening air, perspired; her father
found us, hosing around the greenhouse corner.
I asked after his back, his insomnia (better?).
As we walked off, squeezing, tussling, she
stumbled out her 'Love me forever...'
Come off it! *It's a Barnum and Bailey world/*
just as phoney as it can be,
know that Tracey? She didn't. Was it love then?
Yes, too, with very much romance:
until in her bedroom a lover's accident,
laughing until we shambled in to watch
the supper-show, with
'Mr Izzard, Mrs Izzard...' how-nowing,
end of the evening; walked back.

There was a cat, as I came home
a cat cleaning paws and flanks
delighting, seemed content enough
to eat, sleep and cat; the rats
seemed happy too in hectic scramble, old lunches.
Have been neurotic, all have,
or your Viney gloom as Simon said.
What caper's left, suicide?
No I never intended it.
But the cat seemed doubled-on itself, licking,
intent as the rats making for food,
intent as I, doing what? Slicing my stomach, intent
as the stupid stinging pain of pity.

'Cause pity's pain is not a selfish pain
it's worse. This family,
like it was some ghost town
renewed, sprang living to my
district hospital bedside. Were
all a bit embarrassed, coming
time after time, separately,
(parents that is,
my brother and sister stayed off
after the first time).
Tracey came and Simon,

she crying for a while until,
Simon patting her head, I
asked her 'Please think of me...'
though I suppose
I never thought of them.

I don't recall it hurting
I don't recall much in the least,
except frequent petty picky
quarrels, afterwards their self-
righteous pity; no never
'How could you do this to us etc'
never that, rather a wallow
that they enjoyed their blame.
Oh well, we've all
deserved it, part of the same town,
ghost town, we've shifted now,
the house, a McNab Kurrajong
is being sold to whoever,
the ghost town is over,
except that now we're
all strangers, as I was,
Tracey was. (Could never
ever tell her, she seemed
to like our family.)
Her parents were strange just
strange. No weirdos, but perhaps
she liked a straight run
with us neurotic Vineys.
Mother organizing us as
slices of cake, something,
it all under control
except for Dad, having his
'Gay-and-hearty' and living
and screwing some brainless
bitch I bet, bring her round
Dad, you scared or
something similar?

Oh no-one is mad, Dad's
never found his correct job,
money certainly, but a job, hardly.
Mum's had to balance balance
us, everything. If I'd, we'd,
been treated as bastards,
had something unhappy,
we had the lot yet not the lot,
and I presume, if Dad had a
happy correct job for himself,
it would have been suitable.
But, to condemn the other:
seemed the one concern,
they must have *loved* the idea, once,
those people expendable people,
my trés trés lenient
mother and father full stop.

No one's been asked to hear me out,
what an idea, who'd comply?
Father's out there, careering round to parties,
Mother's surveying all those people,
Tracey...no even if she heard me out
would never understand, she's not
illiterate, as Dad isn't as Mum isn't,
though how can I tell them?
I could recall when I was six or seven,
sitting up late in bed trying
to discern the noises, parents, television
radio, animals, but I don't think I
took the knife, because I sat up
scared when I was six; and don't
bring Tracey into the act! 'I like you,'
I, may be, love her, I'm very fond of her
and don't bring Tracey, she's just a girl
I mean it, look at what she read
before she met me, at times I felt
what a prole! which wasn't fair, I know,
for I met her father
a more civilised old man.

I bite my nails now, it's something,
really a two cent habit. (I'm
writing: Chicken Licken and the sky about to fall.
No it isn't often and likely someone
cuts themselves down at the dunnies.
(It was the sky falling wasn't it,
or the Little Red Hen?)
My childhood terminated hunched up
in Martinson's office, bleeding,
it seems so long ago and
such a mess. Just now,
have heard *My Word* on the radio
when my nerves were a swamp
-origins and derivations-
the stupid Pommy word games,
all comfy, cosy, round the hearth
of a nation, and my mind: flick
flick flick lost patience.
In my Grandfather-built parents'
home, I sat for hours trying
to snuff out thought of Dad or Mum,
their stupid situation, strangers with children.
And then origins and derivations,
how tedious, begetting and begetting
it's biblical! Grand-dad built
and begat and Dad sold and begat,
as I will one day.

Excuse me, all this doesn't happen
every day, I mean one day I'll have
a missus-and-kids (not Tracey)
to regale: how the old man went troppo,
seventeen years old, because his folks
cared more about each other, (yes!)
and really cared. So I'll say *Kids*,
excuse me for paying all this attention
but really your father had a bad time
once, as did his family.
Oh my yes, that's what I'd say,
when I'm old, older, than father is,

mother is, father, mother, parents!
Ahh like it's some ghost town.

Midnight thru dawn

Paul Izzard, the father of Tracey, Brett's girlfriend, a public servant

I may be asked to, as were, round off;
though don't expect *some he did this*
she said that, happy ever after slice, it
will not hold. We've our peeves, fetishes
(so on and so on) might indulge my own
given space, yet there's this Viney caper
that really you know, has to be correct,
in perspective. Therefore dismiss the greenhouse,
lawn-bowls at forty-six, my growing insomnia,
my greater hope of (dare it be?)
clear clean health. Daughter this is your story,
and the Vineys'. Tracey pet it
did upset you didn't it? Whatever he,
strange funny boy, felt and held couldn't,
couldn't be passed over to you.

But you listened *Midnight thru Dawn*
to the *Tom Donnelly Show*, brooded on the tunes,
as if it were your family!
A light shone under the door
and I knocked, entered; your chin hugging
over your knees. Were you 'pondering',
or is that too pretentious?
It's intolerable kids as young as him,
as you should be affected so.
And afternoons all you could do
was amble down the hall at half past five
to watch *Blind Date*.

Tracey, remember when you came into
my small greenhouse one nippy morning, Saturday
it was, fog hemmed around us, you
in a dressing gown, floppy slippers
(a year ago, Autumn as now)
remember? We talked of Brett,
I'd like to meet him of course, when we did

found him aloof, rather intense;
had met his parents once, same table at a school
fund-raising dinner-dance; didn't agree on much,
these people out to sell you something
never have ideas outside your cheque-book.

(But: 'We're going out', what a term, *going out*
or *I'm seeing a lot of*…Cut your hair
soon after, Trace and I was disappointed, though
fashions hardly seem to matter to me now.)

He had a nice sexy wife though, my style, restrained,
charming. She cooled to him as the dinner-
dance continued, he noisier still, not violent.
'Please lift him up Paul, I'm
driving home.' Your mother thought it a cheek,
but I could see it in character and coming.
Out in the carpark he bellowed on
his brother's old club-song, the greater Viney:
and I thought, holding him up, up, the wife
opening the door, I thought: poor pair, there
indeed seems class, she groomed and bossy
who might, but after he had been entered
into the passenger's seat,
she stood, looking over the car
at me, rather embarrassed, but the eyes thanking.

I don't know whether you
loved their son, presumption I suppose,
you never acted moony-eyed, writing
his name on anything, you aren't my
daughter for…see what I mean?
They call us off-beat, as, I trust
you/we are, I am. What a stupid name!
Izz-ard, called Lizard from Grade One
onwards. 'Tracey' I like, so there,
not many of them around; now,
when your mother and I met, Janet
that was the name; what's today's serving
Trudy or Nudey? Tracey's a *name*!

Of course your mother hated it, knew
after eight years you'd be our first
our only Tracey, any Izzard.
Your mother's head seems held in
perpetual migraine, it isn't but
notice how taut around the temples...
wished for more children, wished,
so I can't say your mood after Brett
stabbed himself was like hers,
there seemed confusion yes, yet no despair.
But to say invoke 'See what I mean?'
is high presumption. Why, why
shouldn't you despair, despair again,
receive migraines, lose weight,
on someone who tried to kill himself,
because his parents were what,
weak, no, immature maybe?
I may be asked to as were, chuck
this discourse, if only it wasn't for
you, Tracey, but don't get me wrong,
everything I do isn't always yours,
I have my life in tweed-coat, old green-
fingers in the glass-house.
Exotica? Ahh Tracey just mucking around
with nature. Glad you come out
to see my garden grow on Saturdays.
I liked our talks, my ravings against
the city council, what came after us,
go stupid against developers, their heirs:
faces of the young plump men with those
angular ginger sideburns, assertive eyes, minds
trained to tap a keg; this area
no longer 'began', their jerry-haciendas, patios
and porticos, their wrought iron gates in
gewgaw curls and swirls,
and all squat, if dropped as hay-bales.
I love to hate them, live with them,
work with them, I'm in Vineyland part
of the scenery. Now these go-getters
thanks that they sleep, Bellevue Heights, The Grange,

The Crest, The Panorama, their Karinya Crescent,
well, it's midnight, after midnight now,
twenty-eight nights since you refused
sleep, sleeping tablets, anything, but stayed up,
hugging, as I've said, blankets, listening
to some second-string announcer pump out
Golden Oldies. Thanks that you're asleep now,
everyone is, the Vineys (wherever) your Brett,
your mother, all of Bellevue Heights, all sleeping
except I, the study light on, reading
magazines, and yes listening to
the *Tom Donnelly Show*, chewing over,
What in the hell did they do? Ahh
it's occurring everywhere, praise not here.
I'm too tolerant of argument, to have
my life changed; arguing with her,
reason's the watchword, would all
could use it…*Ramble on, rambling rose*
must be getting tired, for kiddo,
the sun rising is midday and
dusk elsewhere. Oh, I know there's
not much basis in a father's Pollyanna antic
but Tracey it wasn't dreadful, I mean
just your father speaking, I,
clearing the…shit it's a botch daughter
oh Tracey it's all right,
it's all right, everything is going to be, all right.

from
The Nightmarkets

Climbing Up the Ladder of Love

1980. In her late twenties Sue Dobson, an inner-urban Melbourne freelance journalist has become both the biographer and lover of John McTaggart, a well-heeled, womanising, former Liberal Party Minister who now heads a new, increasingly successful middle-of-the-road political party. Meanwhile, hovering about proceedings is McTaggart's one-time lover, party worker Veronica Lim.

Setting: a roadhouse.

The buns look stale, I know the coffee's stewed,
men in tee-shirts, probably tattooed,
mingle and chuckle. But they ignore
a dumpy woman in yellow by the door.
　　　　I've ordered a cup, but this place seems meant
for them and their proud icons: an advertisement
(some model 'chick' devoted to her Mack)
postcards, truck monthlies in a rack,
American number plates, photos of grinning friends,
messages from truckies at the very ends
of Aus: *We're still on the job*
ha ha love Jeff (Tennant Creek) / Sandgroper Bob.
(Accept this as you'd accept their sticker:
'Truckies Carry the Country'. Or don't.)
　　　　　　　　　　　　　　The caf thickens
with families, the drivers up, depart.
I return to my reasons: must make a start
for Koornung.

　　　　　Often with exo the nauseous musk-
like scent recalls last March. I looked out at dusk
while light was clinging to the western clouds,
saw his hills flanked against them.
　　　　　　　　　　　　　'The crowds
are kept at bay tonight, Girl Wonder.'
　　　　Wishing to be polite I held out a number.
Dope? He'd stick to this: something and ice.
Of course, even with the crowds at bay.
　　　　　　　　　　　　Earlier: once, twice,
I'd still my *What are we doing?*

This is bizarre! to puzzle, perhaps halt me; till the ensuing
weeks, months, accumulated and dressed
it in what I thought it could be, or guessed.
Which was? Don't exactly remember but suppose
many things to whatever was required. Oh little 'on-the-nose',
though didn't I understand? Slowly self-esteem shifts
when taking a job he offers, fiddling a compromise on gifts,
and caught between him and yourself
one hour is something the next its opposite.

                                     'He has the wealth,'
advised the gold-digger side, 'use it; go and scoff
at yet another silly male.'

                      Hopeless. So try laughing it off:
'John, I can't possibly accept this blender,
you know drug-crazed, hippy me, it'd all end up
flogged for a habit, yes.' But that wouldn't work either.

        'Return the lot, quit the book, grow up and leave...'
(me as a staunch women's advocate).

        I stayed of course, not exactly to ingratiate
myself into John's world and life, his to mine,
that's the wrong word, make it the company then, which was fine.

        But over a saloon bar hubbub would catch your face on the news.
hearing an acquaintance mutter: 'He's demented...ahh hi, Suze!'

        For when we were launched discretion eased then ceased,
helping friends partake a gossip feast
all Summer till, gorged on scandal the stays
of their manners burst. They swooned on it.

                            Those days
I'd sweep Melbourne like some high priestess
of passion (felt I was tall enough). 'Just guess
who's y'lover?' I'd be found asking.
'Go on, go on.' Spent the next hours basking
in the thought of you. Others never also-ran,
they didn't start! 'The era of the courtesan,'
I'd advise myself, 'quit with button-up boots.
Why so shaky questioning those fruits
of being adult your future and fate is
storing? We've entered the Eighties:
it's *our* decade, what your home and schooling
bred you for. Though the Movement may've quit even cooling

years back, simply to freeze,
it's time any educated woman must seize
her inheritance to all that liberation.
And no use bemoaning this occasion
as transient (they all are) he can, ought to be, is your equal.
Life's not a sequel upon sequel
of boyfriends, their hang-ups and triumphs. Realize you're *not* twenty-three
and some mere boy's girl. You can be me me *me*
at last.' (Though with nothing to trample
over my almost perpetual desire to send it up. Example:
as some tart out of Bangkok or the Levant: '…say meester
I veree sexee, veree cleen…')

By Easter

I was getting driven up to Koornung.
Noon on Thursday a jacket and bag were already flung
into your car, somewhere near Queen Street
and the office. You'd your turn to shout 'Another treat…'
and it was lunch at Lulu's.

Out on the highway I started to puff

a number. He laughed: 'If you've got to smoke that stuff,
wind down the window…' (Laughed but only just, perhaps.)

'Been off it for days…' days I spent researching, and my mind collapsed

to what was on the tape-deck.

'Mustn't turn to a spoiler

and bring work into your holiday Kid, but don't want our book as a pot-boiler,
one's getting churned out for the plebs already, it's half tabloid cartoons…
you listening?'

In a sense yes, but first to the tunes

that filled your car.

Had still to get used to 'staff', with servants, that vainest

of luxuries (your family still retains retainers)
who ignored me. Never felt the housekeeper warming
to 'my biographer', to a euphemism. Why should she?

In the morning

we showered together, then you went to church,
a public duty. I thought of your housekeeper's porch
where a rather scraggy grapevine slumped
round a trellis. But wanting warmth, with hot cross buns I dumped
myself into your study, adjusted the heater,
turned through your photo albums. I'd make them now: what's neater

than an affair in snaps? You'd caught me with a flash bulb
as I awoke that day, yawning, stale and dulled
by too much late night exo, stretching-up to moan as a gorilla:
hair skewed, matted like Phyllis Diller
(I trust not sounding) our day begun
as teenagers might. And weren't we just well done,
recovering from something done well,
for our bed had that close, warm, yeasty smell
of bodies you could almost taste;
had wished to lie for days in it. Knew though how I might be placed
in a continuum of snapped 'ladies',
if heading the heap. Whom he had parading
as fourth or fifth fiddle could always get shuffled
through the pack by that plumage-ruffling
Jack of recent legend. No use dagging
about Koornung when *that* eventuated.

                                True, but not yet. His Party bandwagon
poised to sweep the outer states, he fired
another invitation, which verged on request: 'Sue, it's almost required
you meet my colleagues and organization.' But with a few bugs
to get ironed out: 'Though please, none of these your...' waving a hand, 'your drugs...'
       So May I gave in, Melbourne received a rest,
shuttling with you south, north and west
to rallies; while our affair smoothed-
on into my career: biographer.
                   But needing an aging IUD removed
I'd taken to playing Vatican roulette:
and dickhead! I think now, deserving what you get.
           Thinking: 'It's pest control but Sue as the pest...'
I grabbed a clinic pencil off the desk,
held it out in both hands, and snapped.
We'd our child's course mapped-
back how many hotel/motel suites,
as our adventures turned to endless repeats
of tea-bags, jugs, heaters, shower recesses,
brown brick walls and a sex-drive. (My guess is
Geraldton, Renmark, Tamworth, Toowoomba, Cairns.)
         We wound up in Brisbane. That's where I caught the Party's plans
for Ms Lim's birthday: 'Vron's arriving. Haven't you two met?
I thought you had. A great lady...' though this praise sounding limp, wet,

off-hand. 'She'll coincide with Victory Night.'

The upcoming Saturday
held four by-elections which their mini-campaign
verged on winning (only over-confidence could ruin it)
but I'd seen such smart, cautious tactics as their Policy Unit
kept trucking after like some army kitchen
with all its necessary nourishment.

Yet John was chaffing, itching
for Canberra (of all places!) the House to resume:
'When problems loom, we'll confront that loom!
I'm sure you'll see more than a mere protest vote
against *all* established forces, Clive. Quote,
ordinary Australians don't have to be poked, prodded
into action this time round Clive, unquote.'

The interviewer nodded.

Pundits felt you won a by-election
or two or three through luck. Correction,
more than that, it required quite a quota
of management, and your *better class of voter*
fell to the necessary stratagem.
Right-to-lifers scored you minus ten,
slapped foetus photos on your campaign shops,
heckled, threw fruit, eggs, grappled with the cops.
Covered in cack you grinned like Jimmy Carter:
pro-choice, liberal, reasoned and martyr
for a day, for a campaign.
Linked to these demos opponents would complain,
you answering: '…seems part of a pattern
to me, same shrill thugs…' sensing this would fatten
your swing (as it would). Then greedier
for coverage, you'd shout both print and electronic media
to any dirt dug up about the Right. '…and the Left?
Aren't even truly operating now, they're nix.'

This deft
disposal of my stance, my colleagues,
somewhat jarred. What'd he expect? Che beards, jungle fatigues,
perpetual subversion? Dissent was no less part of the system
than what you'd quit.

Ever since I kissed him

that first time, outside Koornung, John ought to have known
we'd something in common, if just a private life. Could have shown
for *him*, a weird collection of risks
that that entailed. *He* wouldn't have heard half Lygon Street frisk
through our, my love-life, with men I'd refuse spelling out
how Sourpuss Sue, was Starfucker Dobbo, was selling out.

     So this man whose campaign, whose life
I joined, I had to write, arranged for his former wife
to meet me, grant coffee, an interview, near her boutique
in Toorak Road.
          Seems my presence gave their marriage a relief
she didn't understand or want, making her mock-perplexed:
'Goodness! Jack's discovered Women's Lib, whatever next?
Still, glad to see you're not some twitty-crass
tabloid cadet. You've interviewed that Asian lass?
Jack's introduced us, during those days when she'd him *quite* in tow...'
(Really? Another thing that everybody knew *I* didn't know?)
'Politically? I view Jack
as some latter-day school debater. Ask her about this new Jack
though, she'd have less jaundice, less venom.
Him? The socialists? They're the same. Business will suffer and amen
to that I say. Nevertheless, he's chanced himself, his job's on
the line. I can admire that. You're not a Mount Macedon Dobson?'
     Being a Burwood one's enough, at least your ex
feels so. Perhaps he saw me representing my age, class, sex?
Perhaps. It seems now he desired to play like a mull
to my bong; or be some permanent finger-on-the-pulse
informing about what was or could be going on out there. It made one wary,
this desire to *Keep me contemporary*,
I'd slightly send it up: 'Of course. Don't want you to sound dated.'
     So he'd 'Uh-huh' as I kept informing. I was amused. I tolerated.

     All this patience got rather routed
though, meeting Veronica Lim, the once-touted
future spouse and think-tank head. A rival?
She acted so, as if, surrounded by fellas survival
meant being played by who, a Joan Crawford, a Bette Davis?
I wished-out on that, seeing no need to enslave us
in some ongoing performance for *men*, I'd hold

a piece of my peace. Only a nineteen-year-old
could possibly escape with half an hour's strutting, winking
and catty quips.
                          'Think-tank?' I mused, 'Haven't caught many signs of thinking.'
         The State President's Pad: a barrister's mansion on stilts,
where John addressed his victory party: vicious tilts
at the Right, throw-away quips on the Left, that all considered clever,
repeatable: 'Tonight, Australia's politics alter forever:
we've Jacaranda, Grainger, The Valley,
and look at our swing in Eureka!'
                          Shy guys turned pally
to amuse me, for this was work, couldn't afford
to leave my story now. Was I pale? Call it bored.
But how dulled could I remain with a whole book to lurch
into publication? August wasn't it? Call my contribution research,
leave Ms Lim the rest, she no doubt picks up
where I leave off, her kind of cat always licks up
another's cream. Men surrounded her. (Sue, try not to gawk
at your sometime rival who giggles yes giggles.) She's in a time warp,
I saw, those games disappeared with girdles, and sinking
into a cold fury tried not thinking
'I'm better than this, than her...' (which was beneath me
for a feminist) but thought 'So, you've bequeathed me
an old fuck. Well thanks Veronica!' And my self-respect
stopped. Started. Did John, she and their Party expect
face-slapping fireworks and other relics? Not in my day,
though maybe hers, this thinking man's Girl Friday...
Yet even if such portions bore,' I knew, 'love some to last.
This starts my career, it must...'
                          Though was I set to be cast
by John in some 'wilting bloom' role? Did a certain distress
hold me? Had I minded all the travel?
                          'Don't feel like your mistress
yet, if them's the thoughts...'
         No, no they weren't, but told John that the kind of rorts
practised up here were a little wearing: wouldn't get slimmer
if life kept up this permanent progressive dinner,
with barbeques for breakfast, those gladhanding men, their generous cheques
and tropical shirts, who weren't in any way rednecks
please, just not my kind?

Out on the verandah
I met their new Honourable Member for Jacaranda,
chatted him up, a mildly-greenie dentist: ruddy, hoarse
from too much rum and speeches: 'So, you're the girl who charts our
amazing course…'

And later, how very Queensland too, produced his harmonica
for all to join in 'Happy Birthday…dear Veronica'

The sun could still splash, but Melbourne snapped to Winter,
and swaddled in coats, a huge red scarf, Louise would enter
my hallway, check how I was that evening:
'Throat better? Cold going? Not still grieving
over some perfidious man or men? Your health
is too important. Time though I'd an attack of that myself.'

You wouldn't arrive back in your suite till ten. I chanced it.
'John? John? Oh Jack! Jack!' a staffer announced.
'He's somewhere here…' as I thought 'Why do I start flailing
round in your absence? Know the biography's failing.'

'Hope he's still awake,' I'd told Louise,
'John's been busy…' Had to try and breeze-
on into maxi-pathos, being pukka with a heartache,
if it was. No, plain old confusion. Were you awake?
I'd say: waiting to a background of music, babble, the tone
of which seemed *party time! party time!*

You grabbed the phone:
'Hello Central give me Doctor Jazz.'

'Steady John, what you on: Riesling, Mateus, Shiraz?
I'm about to drop a big one, and that portion
of you that's sobre better tune in: we need an abortion.
Not going to chuck a nervy-do, just want your help.'
And I paused, waited, sensing a brief gulp
from over five hundred miles.

'Sue? You all right okay?'
Slurring if concerned.

Oh, who wouldn't give a bouquet,
then, to this year's most sympathetic male?
Supportive promises, desires to '…be with you soon…' couldn't fail,
could they? If Earnest Concern (Theory) were a subject
you'd be post-doctoral: more than a bit suspect
in the practise though. Thanks for little and why bother thanking

for just promises, really? I gave a plus-two ranking
and obsessed my child's course, tracked
it back in my mind till you returned from Sydney.

                                  I was attacked
for being a silly, silly girl, okay, gently chided
for not warning: you were fond, you trusted, you confided
more in me, or so you said, than anyone else.
Therefore 'Whatever I can do...'

                         Oh hallelujah, ring them bells,
this being my first, I trust my last termination, your quota
of platitudes seems endless, quit wooing with them, I'm not a swinging voter.

      And hadn't your progressive image commenced a dud,
in early *Hansards* many words seeming but the cud
of your class: 'containment', 'stock', 'backbone', 'fibre',
couldn't you be quaint (still can: using 'imbiber'
for alcoholic, say, if he's a mate).
Weren't you a PR nightmare, how could your tête-à-tête
with destiny arrive on *that* image?

      You were you said '...pretty Right Sue yes, let's call it Right. It helps me gauge
how far I and Australia have come. Blame my era,
my history, my schooling. Still, the nearer and nearer
I got to power, the more I grew up. Though your Lefties clothe me
in a very middle-of-the-road grey, conservatives loathe me.
I was their own, Seventies-style Stabber Jack.'

                             What's *this* mean?
But a reference explained wouldn't really add, and though you'd still enough sheen
to class you as a 'rebel', was I to discover
a mere question of ambition, no votes in yet another lover
how discreet or advertised?

                    I was. Soon after, lying awake
in yet another Motor Lodge, we ordered a break:
'quarter time' as it was neatly termed;
saw a landslide defeat if your effort of concern
were politics. By then I wouldn't want you to intrude,
for even asking 'Sue, what's up?' seemed a platitude.

      Yet of course I liked you, but needing to cope with the warp and weft
of what we term 'relating', this wasn't just another girl out of her depth,
probably worse, a woman, and spent nights hunting
for excuses, even reasons. Knew I was stunting

myself with tantrums, trying hard
to avoid them, not wishing to drop my guard
and screech 'Fuck off!' like when you were grazed
by an attempted cuff, later admitting 'Sorry, I was fazed...'
a word that shamefully I can't abide.

      Or sweat-banded we jogged, each at the other's side,
panting like pups. What's *that* ever prove?
Sport at the third remove,
hearing your kind of Debbie-Dollies in the changing-room: 'Garth reckons
my tracksuits are straight out of Fabulous Seconds,
and he *still* won't believe the labels!'

      Could I believe yours? How could I trust to trust your babble
or my own? May have had your Life to finish, an agility
to sometimes keep my counsel, now though I was your liability.

      Throat like an oven, phlegm like toffee,
those mornings Lou was busy, but Ian came: 'Earl Grey? Coffee?'
      Tea thanks, and he'd chat with mummy me trussed
into two pullovers and gown. Lunchtime she'd arrive and they'd fuss
like parents. (Come on, will you coy two ever stoke
this easy eyeing-off into a relationship?) Had croaked
'Just run down with a chill...' two days before. More than mere chill
now, I'd flu oh flu the great! and my book could stand still
forever. Lou phoned his office, my notes were packed,
and the deadline transferred to, well, whoever.

                        Pillows stacked
behind me, sun through the window, how was tricks?
My Kleenex mountain grew, I stank, like the room, of Vicks,
but felt improving. Saw them to the door, came back to my damn erratic
disease, whatever I had. 'Call it psychosomatic...'
I mumbled, fell asleep then half awoke, still dressed
in sweat first, clothing a sticky second. Would've been depressed
about my, our whole dumb business
but had this great distraction of an illness
distancing me from you. Couldn't see how some amends
might be adjusted though. After all my problem-lobbing onto friends
was Ian impatient, Louise annoyed
helping my emotions get easier employed?
Their suffering friends a terrier
for digging out one more disaster area.

Never been a type to sigh 'So be it…'
yet just look every hour, you'll see it:
a juggernaut marked *fate* is easily hitched
as one woman's destination is switched
for another's. Could call it 'control'
if you like or 'playing some role',
but one never should: you're never a 'role'. However erratic
the mind or heart gets, life's not amateur dramatics.

      With this 'trial separation' didn't greatly
care, got blasé, anything happen lately?
Haven't seen you in weeks! Been turning chubby, as diets, fitness
start tomorrow and always did. But things improve, witness
how we've moved our drinking: dealers, junkies have poured
into the Albion and stayed. Making me bored
at the least, they've washed us down to Fitzroy
and The Standard. It's my life, why shouldn't I employ
such reference points? You've your Club, with Lulu's or the Lobby
where to tryst, and since dining with you has swung from hobby
to career now, please take other women to impress.
                                   For something hackled,
as grit got in our friendship I didn't wish to be shackled
with someone calling me *Kid* just once too often
and just accept such irritations, having to soften
them with the excuse of your sex, age and class, for that old latent cat
in me merely to purr, refuse to scratch.
                              It began as a chat,
just gossip. I was a fool of course, yet wasn't, to go pumping
you on the ins 'n' outs of political bed-jumping.
Harmless enough trivia, wasn't ready to ensure
it'd get me wincing or worse. Yet now no colours seem truer,
and wouldn't I crawl that clichéd mile
of shattered glass to view the leader with his shy if warm smile
swapped for the grin some sexist smarty:
'Sue, haven't I said we've affirmative action right through our party?'
      So shutting you down with all such tokenist stunts,
'Please,' I asked, 'don't look so goddam hurt.'
                                And once,
when you'd another album out for the showing:
'Vronnie and I had this thing going…'

(Going? And hadn't it *gone*?) 'Well before I met you
well before. Not jealous?'

                        Would never let you
turn me into some stereotype, would I? Can't demand her
sacking on my account but 'John, I can't stand her!'

        Wasn't prepared for analysts though, to join the legions
of those 'meaningfully depressed', patrolling their regions
of therapy and medication. Any fool has power to grope-
on through the murk, given faith enough to cope,
adjust and continue, take a finger, dab it
in spit then test the air: 'Oh John? He's an ex-habit
sure, but I'm weaned off.'

                      Then early mornings
I'd awake, recovering from dreams, their warnings
of what to avoid (or should have) had risen, burst-
through then flowered to seed again. Was the worst
I still could be your lover if required,
still the girl on tap? I'd been so wired
for changes, call it hormones, call it 'Your late twenties/early thirties fog…'
(Ian's phrase) a suitable one since those Winter weeks seemed clogged
with a greyish, indecisive nothing. Now, with little to repeat,
all combinations having occurred, I considered playing Susan, Duchess of
                                      Lygon Street:
part mistress, part biographer, yet always the favourite.
Though how could I take *intimate* as in '…then we became *intimate*…'
if it meant 'being this close' to Australia's latest, would-be pretender?

        Drovers, miners, abalone-divers hit town, go on a bender
and, if so much creeps up grey, ill defined, to confuse
like then like now, I also head to pub company. Tends either to amuse
or bore, and when these overlap keeps reminding
me how Lou once said: 'Maybe it *is* this mind thing,
but Melbourne! On occasions I've heard and agreed, or thought and said myself
Fuck fuck fuck. In this place do they think of nothing else?'
        So chatting-up one Friday at The Standard,
after a joint has hyped me ultra-candid:
'Like getting smashed, Kev? I do. Wine, lager, bitter,
draught, even stout? Nah. Spirits only tonight.'

                      The hues of winter
filled the public bar: blacks, blues and browns;

with friends to share my ups and ride my downs
I'd arrived back. And this Kev deserved I make a start
in 'getting along'. But the taste was tart
and I shuddered, saw myself staring in
a barrel of bullshit, all that's (so called) egalitarian.

      A Women's Studies postgrad meets a wharfie/
painter-and-docker/that ilk, say, invites him back for coffee,
a number, a rave. And what's to follow
the next day? 'Bonjour Kev.'
                  'Huh?'
                        'That's hello
in French.'
          And the final hour is spent
trying to save him/you more embarrassment.
      Oh a touch of the worker and consciousness unfurls
to separate the women from the girls,
they think. Poor deluded molls, why slave
after ockers? Haven't you heard they've
almost another language? Why bumming it
round public bars for even further slumming it?
Sure there's a whole class struggle to instil 'em
with, but you just wince with every 'haitch' and 'fillum'.

      Yet I am sure how they feel these guys,
floundering beyond an un-used-to-depth somehow applies
to my last year. Only now has the in-house rebel
returned to discover her own level:
not having to explain the unspoken
(since such shouldn't get explained, as token
of a similar wavelength); *not* having to always chat, discuss,
argue, or when things got truly arch, rap.
                        'You're a stubborn cuss,'
would be announced, '...a liberal education, still you won't budge,
much.' (I'd adapt more if this less-than-subtle nudge
towards what you believe wasn't so constant.)
Then I truced, supposing we acknowledged similar problems, while you'd grant
my interesting theories: '...though the practice, the practice!'
      Even this part of our game wouldn't last, became quite seasoned in kiss-
and-make-up, just like in them fillums. It still amazes
being your lover (you mine) reheating your phrases:

'…can't keep my hands away…aren't we just a couple of sooks…'

Today I'll be arriving with those papers, books
loaned for my work, and I'm thinking: 'Play cool, Koornung could tee you
another afternoon like all the rest.' Thinking: 'Love to see you,
want to but don't need to…' the chorus of what I choose
to call my present reverie: Roadhouse Blues.

For I mean you weren't just a novelty. It would inflame
some that I haven't yet quit in disgust, or don't proclaim:
'*His* pack? Little but a mob of trendies…' Trendies?
A meaningless term of abuse which in the end is
merely repeating the old old Left honing-
in on 'Silvertails.' And no use moaning
The establishment the establishment!
in your case, whose influence is spent, spent,
clunk and over. With old wealth a museum piece
only its pride remains, though that's enough to stop you greasing
up to the media magnates…yet.
Respecting (if not you) your families, their debt
is owed to a tone, but then it stops.
For what's a use of Buvelots, riding crops,
restored jinkers etcetera with laser technology? Crown, sceptre, orb
of a quaint past; just like graffiti the Movement daubed
during the Struggle. Did we *Lynch McTaggart*
a decade ago? We did, and I tell myself 'You've just to hack it,
sweetheart, each time his past, our present, whose future
is presented.'

'That clown'll suit ya,'
a friend said, 'like a leper.'

Some friend!
Was proud to ditch *her*, proud not to pretend
what had our affair become; or so I thought
for some things had escaped: *Jack Mac's Biographical Rort*
was a smutty par sub-headed *Ssshh (Hot!) Gun Wedding Chimes?*
Yet alluding sniggers in *The Toorak Times*
merely pestered, knowing they'd never hold a candle
to any all-star celebrity affairs. Can't see this as any 'scandal'.
Melbourne might adopt group apoplexy,
I'll not bother.

But know how our afternoons can build: slow, sexy
and, if we'd admit most loving, to find us snarling,

grunting as some sow and hog. Why ask 'Fuck me...' when 'Fuck me darling...'
sounds that much better, hitting this woman *just there*.
Mere words mightn't commit you, but surely you're aware
even these smallest touches add, cement
a couple's feelings. Oh there's friends who'd have me repent
at the term 'couple', but knowing you I've learnt
enough guile and gall to quip 'What were we if we weren't?'

        Yet I've re-joined my crowd: those art, Rock, writing, acting, teaching
                                  mentors
of the inner-urban Left. My morning centres
yet again on coffee, coffee and hearsay; and starting
yet again on other people's business, around Carlton
what's not up for belief, the gossip seems so numerous.
        Though yesterday a very queen of rumours,
whose source is excellent: I head...ahem!
the job short-list at QED-FM.
Imagine this: Sue hosting current affairs
(might have *you* on) coordinating live-to-airs,
all purpose two IC. Oh, it'll serve to give
a public what they crave: quite alternative,
quite my style and generation.
                The other night when Lou and I were stoned
(first time after a few months break) you phoned,
with news hoping to enhance
my name, your life: *Another Choice, Another Chance*
by Susan Dobson and Veronica Lim.
Thanks, but I'd not been asked by any her or any him
to be included.
        'And who,' I asked, 'thought up that title, sweetee?
It'll sure look grand on my curriculum vitae.
Vron 'n' Sue, eh? You've a fine pair of intellectual minders.'
        'Kid, you're recognition's deserved, it's at the binders...'
        Which may've helped my aim to laugh it
off and into: 'Please John, something must've been worth it,
say something is or was...' But I didn't, knowing I rank quite poorly
in the tact ratings.
        Though something could be salvaged, surely,
even this afternoon? Don't want it frittered
into sitting at this table littered

with plastic knives and forks, fast-food bibs.
So I sip my coffee, prepare to meet His Nibs
(my pendant wearing, slight-greying Mr Bliss)
thick-sconing myself into the obvious:
you were my prize and I yours,
but match abandoned am writing off the scores.
That's civilised and ex-lover deferring to ex-lover
how it should be.
              'Michelle!' And a young mother
snaps, her five-year-old messing in a bin
sending her ratty. 'Michelle!' She gives the world a din
of 'Don't, don't, don't!' I'd do it too.
The child gets smacked.
              Study the table Sue.
Michelle! It must've been unfurled
by now on half of a half of the English-speaking world,
poor brat (hardly more than five) a freckled, roly-poly
kid in cardigan and floral skirt. Some names digest slowly
through time; I think though this one's stuck.
                    But neither too 'normal'
(Lara, Tara, Samantha, Danielle) nor too 'formal'
(Emily, Emma, Sophie, Sarah) Bronwyn's a fine, strong name.
And maybe I've headed to another hobby horse to entertain
a thought of a future Bronwyn Louise?
And if I have? There might be a tight squeeze
in my schedule but give five years, well into some career
(QED as mere stepping stone) I might've bred, though this could appear
as maybe less, if any worthwhile partner's found.
      And he'll hear-tell things about you, aware how the scripts, sight
                        and sound
of a public-figure ex-lover still remain.
                  And so one night, as interlude,
behold McTaggart once more on the tube.
And my husband/boyfriend/the child's father might laugh:
'Weren't you once a member of his staff?'
        'Euphemisms become you,' I'll reply, always geared
for this quiet, slightly caustic man with a beard
to make his brief sardonic comments. Four years my junior
he'll have this point-scoring concern: 'Miracle is you weren't ruined
absolutely, Sue…the clown's demented.'

And knowing I won't object quits there. He's meant it,
but that can't hurt. You were jobs away, Bronwyn ago.
What started as a 'profile', turned you companion, employer, beau
for ten (what a hoot!) months.
                                   And you'll gather,
John, I'll be capable of saying it, then.
                                   After the Weather
he suggests we watch what follows, but though on leave I'm tired, Bron
                                                 must be fed.
The Late News flickers to a dot, out. We go to bed.

from
The Lovemakers

Cross QC: Three Villanelles

for Michael Prideaux

(i) R v Kent: The cross-examination

> ...after what's been said and what's been done
> it distresses, I understand, this evidence.
> Let's get it right though: *then* he dropped the gun?

> A criminal shot, a colleague dead, just one-on-one:
> life's never been like this before, it's far, far tense
> than any courtroom, right? Yet, after what's been done,

> after you've heard *I'm gonna get you, son...*
> please constable, take no offence
> but get it right: he dropped the gun

> and then he aimed it? Where'd you read that? *The Sun?*
>   (Your Honour I withdraw.)
>   But what amount of sense
> does this make: after all's been said and done,

> with a partner dying wouldn't you make a run?
> (The only thing left to prove your innocence
> is time.)
>   And yet Kent doesn't. My client drops the gun.

> What guilty men act this way: lots, a few, none?
>   (When a life's at risk all words swell immense,
> soon as they're said.)
>   As for what was done:
> we have it right? *Then* he dropped the gun?

(ii) R v Kent: The summing-up

> The case you've heard, with due respects, is bent.
>   We may not like him, think he's highly flawed,
> yet he's stayed calm my client Mr Kent,

and that's but a start to show he's innocent.
            Up rose his hands as he howled *Oh Gawd!*
(the case you've heard unravels, it is bent)

having a good idea what *Drop it!* meant
but, for a second froze: his being gnawed
with staying calm.
            My client Mr Kent's

no saint (what chassis never had a dent?)
It's hardly the point he gambled and he whored
with due respects.
            The case you've heard is bent:

relive this evidence again: the scent
of anger's out, the ground is being pawed...
still he stays calm my client Mr Kent

Four! Five! Six! That gun was a long time spent.
Throw it down! somebody implored.
And didn't he?
            The case you've heard is bent:
for he stayed calm my client Mr Kent.

(iii) Some hours after the execution

            I wish I'd had his strength.
                        Now, calm as he was
they've a stronger, calmer Kent to bury
(*perhaps* and *maybe* shall give way to *because*).

            My job requires plain speech, if no applause,
but how could you notify a jury
I crave the strength and calm I thought was

his; how most nights dreaming of rowing I haul through mud the
                                                oars
of a middle-aged barrister in a hurry?
            Our *perhaps* our *maybe* turned *because*

shaking hands a week ago: 'Thanks Mr Cross.
Had I the know-how I'd syphon off a brewery
and pay you in grog for life.'
                              Calm as Kent was

he knew *doubt* as our one escape (all other doors
were boarded up) knew it had been a puree
of *perhaps* and *maybe*, to taste but once, because

if we have the crimes we have the laws
and have now, the premeditated fury
of revenge.
                Today, stronger than even Kent was
(*perhaps* dying and *maybe*) the State has demanded *because*.

Roger, or Of Love and its Anger

for Phyllis Webb

> *And yet I shall have to do something.*
> *Ah, the key of our life, that passes all wards, opens all locks,*
> *Is not I will, but I must. I must, – I must, – and I do it.*
> Arthur Hugh Clough *Armours de Voyage*

1 Chez Charley

Who hasn't seized on that urge to dump it
and snarl *Mop this, Charley, disinfect the stink!?*
But Charley's hardly my darling, he's my shrink.
Likeable enough, the man's not one to trumpet
symptoms, causes and cures (nostrums for what life
is or isn't) as I am less than a dead-set cert
psychotic with overabundant traumas to blurt
upon Dr Charles Bell FRANZCP. Were I some housewife
(to be charitable, older style) trying to rid
herself of what she's become, I might cross-refer
to such tableaux as nappies soaking in their trough,
toast staling on its breadboard.

                             Well whacko-the-did!
For Roger has to hang his jacket of despair
upon the hook of what, mmm? Just nothing and the lot.

2 This

'Our marriage,' Charley hears, 'seemed as nurtured, caressed,
as...' I consider *Or so I thought* but shirk
cueing it in. 'The thing, dammit, worked!'

            'How come then,' he asks, 'after such a harvest
you're left with the pips, the pith, the rind?'

            No question is newer, no question seems older.
For a reward I tell him how I told her
what facts I wanted known. Time then to rewind:
why'd this occur: the this of 'this' and the 'this' of *'this'*?

            After such close-ups therapy zooms back and pans
out to a declaration. 'Oh little equals that nearly-

enough sober passion I have for her…anything amiss?'
My slow smile baits.

And 'Roger!' the man's
guard-dropping, 'Roger, come off it, really!'

3 Grammar Lesson

It was about then I sensed him: Neil.
(Of course the name came later.)
And meantime, coining verbs (to partially-hate-her/
to even-forgive-him) I began to feel
how, better and better I now knew my wife. Funny,
the items that were realigned till, whatever got purged
bloomed into an exhilaration as each suspicion surged
into the next new verb: e.g. to be-taken-for-the-bunny-
I-never-thought-I-was. Except I was; whilst the inanity
of being-somewhat-jealous got dumped in with the hoi-polloi.
After that power of *Roger! Barbara! Neil!* what would verbs prove?
Yet, though I'd done with them, my vanity
released into another: to Wonderboy;
and I knew she had a lover, was a lover, was in love.

4 The Wonderboy Variations

Though someone never met, never seen,
allows us still to improvise our bit
Rog and Barb and who…what, please, should come between
this three of us?

Fold-dovetailing-fold here is the fit:
if someone's leaving, someone's taking over
and when I'm lukewarm you'll be undoubted hot.
Then after test-running sarcasm, *Lover,*
I sighed, *here we are and not,*
Wonderboy my three-dimensional shadow
see how we weave, how we duck and feign!

Barb and I ate out. And given an hour to toy
round with the kari laksa, mee goreng, gado gado:
'He's who? Who?'

'Neil. Just Neil. Just a name.'
And just-a-names just help eh, Wonderboy?

5 Sorry

Roger's tears were dammed. There are those myths
that knit us into families and he, trying
to invent a further few, saw no percent in crying,
only this need: to step back from the Heaths
in their marriage, its warp and weft,
and behold!
　　　　　　After a dose of them's-the-breaks
(them's ideals shedding like eczema flakes)
he took himself to a whorehouse, but left.
Its intros were amusingly percussive,
offsetting the lingerie: *I'm Lee-Ann I'm Jess*
I'm Chelsea I'm Starr.
　　　　　　　　　Cows moo, ducks quack
and 'Sorry,' was heard from Rog, 'never enough of a spiv.'
　　　And later, when nerved to scan the contact press,
what hit him more, its tragedy or tack?

6 Roger and Ray

'Chrissie's adventurous, don't tell her but. Floating
are we? She's nice, says I'm a bit of a hack
in the cot, but honest.' (It hardly seemed gloating,
they'd hunt out floaters, bring them back:
Honey meet the World…the World, Hon…) 'Ever watched
yours at it? Mine?' His eyebrows raised:
'No mate?' sighing, proposition botched.
　　　'That's novel,' I offered, passing it for praise
that he misheard.
　　　　　　　'You're *writing?*'
　　　　　　　　　　　　I smiled.
'Possibly…' as good a line to help intrigue
my present lot (or his or hers).
　　　　　　　　　Wouldn't douse
that afternoon in Chrissie, but seeing him so beguiled
by the world and his wife, next time, in league
with curiosity perhaps, I'd check it, meet the spouse.

7 Roger and Chrissie (i)

I saw them as my kind of couple-
you-meet-on-holidays (there seemed no-one else)
though Ray's motives rang more bells
than a cathedral. Sarcastic? I was doubled
over. Like *Douches a User's Guide* or *Where to Graze
in L.A.* we were magazine fodder,
and 'open' or otherwise I tried to prod her,
tenderly, out of marriage.
                                 Some days
we drove somewhere, sat, kissed,
exchanging similar enough plots: how a whim
can bloom into commitment. Then as her throat unloaded
sobs, I held that darting-mousey face: 'Chris, Chris...'
(turning shrink/director/coach) 'stop doing this for him!'
          The wailing would cease; softly under my hands she exploded.

8 Roger and Chrissie (ii)

We're still *us* with added rider *just*,
and if this mightn't be exactly love
it's believable. (Hoping to be a cut above
hypocrisy our motto's not *Fidelity or Bust*.)
Then, since she says how fine, tip-top, okay
Chrissie's feeling, to stymie potential pouting
we hit a film: Americans are shouting,
always have been. (Though Rog and Barb and Ray
and Chris seem little better than the soaps tut tut.)
          In last night's dream *us* with our Red Setter
just jogged some forgettable foreshore, and indeed
what fantasies aren't as disposable?
                            But, big but,
'Roger,' her eyes still say (no eyes say it better)
'I need you, need you, need you, need...'

9 Eyes

After Barb's spillage of his name and history
made me know I could feel second best,
and since I'd been quite enough a guest
at my proposed defeat, I saw no mystery
to solve. Just hunt the parallel that fits.
This day's been either some Outer screaming 'Carn!'
I thought, *or with her contained response pavane-*
like. And I'm thankful, given both it's
how she tells her truth.
But Barbara's eyes
were shut. 'You had her candid,'
the lids informed (near enough to bricks
commandeering window space) 'accept how such a prize
she's had to be.'
Events hedging a mean, a standard,
let's focus said pavane upon domestics.

10 Games

Believing *this still works* we waved-
off any love; learning to redeploy
such passion left, we iced it. All faults caved-
in, accommodating whoever.
Wonderboy
say, what was his name, his name…
Waldemar…Boris…Ahmed…Chuck?
It gets to be a game beyond mere game.
You rove, okay, just keep me in the ruck.
Or my turn, Chrissie: three wooden brooches
chorus-lining a lapel, pragmatic smart
and pleasantly abrupt, lean hips
tatted with butterflies.
Each lover coaches
for the next. Beyond mere game lies art.
These are the way you have relationships.

11 Fifteen Minutes

Thinking to go out again I shaved
and, so used to the sound any shower
makes slapping onto her, never gave
it my mind: one more quarter hour
of marriage, except, taking this punt
she stepped over the bath, flicked her
eyes my way. What did we want?
Something neither could predict or
didn't have to.
Another defunct
affair was closing.
Frame some rules because
Charley there must be rules. One-through-ten
tonight were concertina'd thus: don't get
used to your lover (whatever he was).
Looked as if she needed me again.

12 The Heaths (i)

We met at a wedding minus my 'and friend'
(this mate's sister who'd snaffled out a virus)
with a requisite summer evening to fire us
into kissing. At that age, when the means and end
seem one, you'd think I'd try for more; instead
we merely pashed. Next night I took her out
and given a week it never looked in doubt
we'd find ourselves, somehow, in bed.
Barb still tells what each other wore,
as if from then she was in training
for nostalgia. And though my cast is wider (the result's
most of my life) it's premised on this necessary lore:
we made each other happy; little needed explaining;
nothing seemed difficult.

13 The Heaths (ii)

Love for that age has neither rules nor regs;
the intimate was there to be seized
for nothing was less infinite. Being so pleased
at becoming *us*, we would (with her Grade Six legs,
my hardly-any pecs)
gift-wrap the normal, dump the exotic back on its pallet.
Blunt as filigree, delicate as a mallet
that's the charm of good old s.e.x.
Which I sort of *got* one day.
                    So I kissed her
by my car (proposing a rendezvous,
a continuation) ever on our slight alert
for the arrival of friends, her folks, a sister.
         That summer all we had to do
it seems, was lift her skirt.

14 The Heaths (iii)

The question was its answer; with 'Yes,' a parent asking,
'but what can you *know*?'
                    And tempted to say
The alpha and omega of s.f.a.
I surely shrugged, all the time basking
in that sweet reflected shock of *living together*.
Though two youngsters tipped into a vat
of compromised excess, we'd hardly considered *that*
and would agree to well…whatever:
circles dotting your 'i's and 't's crossed with swirls,
invite the planet!
                    As I coached my teeth
to tighten through some glass-charged MC lurch-
ing-forth his *Ladies and gentlemen, boys and girls,
be up standing please…meet Mr and Mrs Heath!*
'…we'll do it,' said her mother, 'at the church.'

15 The Heaths (iv)

Sprung in a diary or a panel van
there's little kids prefer to getting caught
(unless of course it's nothing of the sort,
which wasn't us). After we made Sam,
or given our dilemma found we had,
I started a word-search. The night
he arrived it stopped: perfect…correct…? No, *right.*
That Barb and Rog became Mum and Dad
seemed as simple, plain. And call it Straight Pride,
but there, for preference, went those closets
we'd never need. Or consider how lucky
we still are. But *for preference* I could've joined that tide
of men who sweep on North (glands cooking up deposits
of Oz) for plenty South East Asian fucky-fucky.

16 The Heaths (v)

So a friend might return and, in an aside,
tell of some girl from Denmark or Illinois.
Which gave Barb the breach: 'But you're a good boy!'
I loved and won't forget the one-time child-bride
raising her eyebrows to send our guest flailing-
free: 'We toured a bit…I'd hardly call us lovers.'
'What, just one, Andy? Surely there were others!'
(As if on our behalf she was saying
Well, we're adults now.)
And, as he volleyed the taunting:
'More? Of course there were!' Andy's reserve bent
to her cheek, her charm.
'And okay what,' I joined our tease
'gives in those so-called bars?'
Though if the theme's jaunty-
enough (near to a decade old) here's today's variant:
There weren't others, just him, that one, Neil…please…

17 Grit (i)

Strange, though my pain has melded into top shelf
restraint, its message stays this elemental:
I know where you've been…going to tell myself
on you… Yet if the game's that parental
who then is the parent? Together
with everyone we'd devised this clomp-clomp
choreography: one special pas de…whoever.
If that's how adults dance bring back the Stomp,
I say or said, still sufficiently in awe
of what is possible, with no desire to identikit
me as some martinet, addict, abuser.
But oh, when did the grit arrive, that flaw
which, although I hardly knew it
then, was steadily turning me loser?

18 Grit (ii)

It won't square with ladies, but getting decked
is a compliment; if you can hit and be hit
so can he. When fighting implies a certain respect
why thump your loathed one? (It's better to spit.)
Wonderboy deserved neither. If hardly innocent
his acts were love-fuelled.
                              As if direct from the shit
of battle I wished I could've signalled this opponent
You and Barb…d'd'dit dardardar d'd'dit…
don't send reinforcements just rest my fears
and tell me why.
                    So exit thoughts of 'Put up y'dooks.'
Today's far more a case of this: combs raised and fighting fit
two more Chanticleers
strut respective barnyards (mine, Wonderchook's)
pecking into their wondergrit.

19 Roger's Dream

…and the grit was love, love or her need/
my want, which doubtless approximated.

So, had he that just-enough ardour to free her,
briefly, from our growing up? Me, I never hated
any two the less, though the tears wept
were milked by Barb Heath and her Boy Scout,
and for years I've conjured, though hardly slept
through, Roger's dream.
                              Whilst the household's out
a man passes into my home: he's no thief,
hardly touches a thing, but *These are their books*
he notes, *they've made their beds like this.*
        We'll never meet, so what could be the brief
of any shadow-boxed defence, when violence is for sooks
and only my want informs me he exists?

20 Anger

        So maybe she needed him, but to fall
once, then fall for the falling so it would gel
into obsession, now that's betrayal
and I am confessing Charley: to tell, re-tell
of love and its anger: the flame, how we fan it
into a blaze. Risking small chaos, smaller harm,
he'll seize his pain, seek to inform the planet
a full parades-worth: that's the charm
of an angry man. What's better breached
than despair? Where's passion better lodged
than with, let's say it, truth? When rage is spilt
rehearsals still wait to get preached.
Barb I wanted to ask her, *we've dodged*
our fears enough, let's have them killed.

21 Love

        But hate is never the risk love is; and I shall love.
        There are those who, sliced to the quick-of-it/
shying from the thick-of-it,
demand (not even the odd kid glove)
nothing but the barge pole option. They're allowed.
My life has just one law: somehow I must
keep this faith: she took me and I her, on trust;

till we more than lashed that braying crowd
predicting our demise, we made this: our family and its home.
It has to have been love, what else frees you from errors
you're meant to commit? Oh my wife might sling me cheek
(and I tolerate this as I always will the foam
of Barb) but she knows I'll never get conned by the terrors
of failure, seduced by their bravado and mystique.

22 React!

      An open marriage? An open sesame
on those bones in my, your, anyone's attic?
Ever accommodating (didn't need to impress me
but Neil had) and ever pragmatic
(want someone else…then he's that someone else!)
I mapped him through her:
whether they danced on asphalt or eggshells,
mock-honeymooned in Eden or a sewer,
I could attune and wait, as 'React!' Barb simmered,
'Fuck you Rog, react!'
                  Well some men
cry, some men laugh, some put it in writing,
and I can't forgive but could forget, since the winner's
moi! But if all happens (as it all happened) again:
I'll tell them Charley as I told her, he's fighting.

23 'How Affairs Succeed'

      For no-one reads an article or book
to think *Yes, that's the way to run it.*
At least I don't. Those reasons some *Cosmo*-hack
gives in 'How Affairs Succeed'? We'd all begun it
whatever *it* was, generations before.
The early-to-mid twenties of this family man
slotted into an inevitable mosaic, sure;
but Barb liked me. She never per se planned
to share another's words, breath, body, farewell-kisses,
which seemed the silliest events on earth,
at the time. For me simple *going at it*
wasn't simple. I'd other ways to please the missus

if not excite her. Don't try them? Then you're not worth
that pinch of the proverbial. No, something better mattered.

24 'the moon of your marriage'

Yet, she's seeing someone. Doesn't need a barrage
of love-bites to be hit, for one more crater
to pock the moon of your marriage.
Oh you'd always hear from clever men, years later,
what they would do: stay very single, forget
if any kids were ever hatched.
But Barb, I and Sam lived what we had for *that?*
Pragmatics are too passionate. Try it detached
and you'll still need to conceive (italics/
capital H) *Him.* Enough contenders bound
from the blocks, most you'll never meet (the price
of a good imagination). This issue, the smart alecs
know, requires a more soluble state. They pound
the problem (yes you have one) with advice.

25 Man-to-man

So when friends mind your business it's an art
to wear their blunt moralising
Man-to-man Rog, you married a tart.
A skill, sure, like Barb disguising
not *Him* but her despair: the hocus-pocus
affairs need to continue. (Or love, who knows?)
I'd get myself asleep hardly rousing notice
at the hour she might return, stoned I suppose.
By spring Barb seemed caged to the haywire pulley
of infatuation. Near Christmas she came clanging
back: their trysts, assignations, dates
had closed. And I'd the future: enough to sense *bully-
the-lot-of-it*: sharing her round, hanging
out for what's thought martyrdom, by mates.

26: The Heaths (vi)

       Since most times we'd adjust. Those nights I'd end
on some past-the-heel edge of the city...
or her quotation marks round 'catching up', 'friend...'
were fugues curling out and back to routine.
                                  Self-pity?

Less happier men can't tell themselves
She's fucking this guy it doesn't matter much
because I say this someone else
is only lucky now... (He was as clutched
to what us kids, for we were kids, believed,
and that was passing.) *...with all their perks*
of love a highly probable grand finale
approaches.
         So much for those ghosted entries heaved
into *Open Marriage: How It Works.*
I never over-dupe myself on books, Charley.

Sophie

197–

Towards the end of school I asked a friend:
'Wouldn't you love to bring your mother home
someone truly vile, someone you'd been with
half an hour before? And stand there,
glowing?
      My friend said 'No...' and
'What are you running on?'
      Should I have answered
No-one hits a girl quite like a mother hits her?
or *I mean, when you're sixteen and a mother hits you?*
      Need we talk about it: a family in collapse,
our better schools, the house at Lorne, careers
and career changes, everyone in love with the guilt?
      Whatever they used to write novels about,
isn't there something more important around?

Ades

      When I was with Karl he wanted to know
all about my family, said he was
a family junkie.
      He'd heard of Dad, of Dad
and Adrian.
      When he's nineteen someone at
his club announces: 'Ades, you're nothing but
a sports star.'
      Adrian is a dog
and this is his bowl.
      Does Karl know how Adrian
does crazy things with crazy women?
He will soon: halfway through our next party
my brother's off with some ridiculous nurse,
first to the Lorne house, then right along
the Great Ocean Road.
      These are the times, this is what they are.

Trophy

       When I'm eighteen and a waitress,
Christian arrives at Pizza X.
Looking at me he's looked at in return.
(Though when I mention him it's all prefaced with
'Well, apart from the bodyshirt…)
       Then he says 'When we're out together
don't bend over too much. Have to hold back
the hordes, won't I?'
       Am I to think he means it?
Christian means a lot of things.
He does karate proud and as for Zen
reckons he understands it.
       He loves the way my ringlets have been done
and thinks he 'gets' me.
       Aren't I Sophie the trophy?
                   He'll have to do.

Black belt

       That January I walk out on mother
and go to Christian's unit.
               I study Law.
       Thursdays and Fridays though, he drops me off
at Pizza X.
       He's eight years older.
He doesn't drink and one night
I am drunk enough to bait him:
'Loosen that black belt, Christian!'
       So I am hit.
           He's sorry
but at times he'll hit again,
thinking in his arrogance I can be trusted,
trusted enough to stay.
            Girlfriend and cash,
he'll leave both lying around;
deserving one another they leave together.

Boyfriend

If Christian ever finds me
Daryl won't save me from Christian.
Yet I have Daryl now. He has a pretty cowlick.
His father wants him as a solicitor.
He'll try, although he'd rather be a chef,
at least. All the time he laughs.

A Regular

We try living in the hills,
and then attempt communal houses
closer to town.
                In one place a regular
is Karl: eight years older than us
with his deep, black beard.
        He says things like
'Too yuppie to be hippy, too hippy to be yuppie…
meet the Podes!'
                I am not a Pode,
my husband is: Daryl Pode, chemist's son from
Templestowe, Ivanhoe Grammar old boy.
        So our household meets the Podes,
who have suspended Law to try out for
Gourmet Grub to Go, their catering game.
        When Karl calls Daryl 'Commander Quiche'
I like it though I shouldn't.
I'm laughing but I can't stand Karl.
And I am not a Pode.

Lawyers

I had summer classes but Daryl was ecstatic:
he, the household and some mates were following
Eddie and The Niddries *Eating the Hand that Feeds You*
national tour.
                'Good,' I was encouraging, 'good…'
being on Pode overload: Daryl's cowlick,
Daryl's giggle, Daryl whom Sophie married

to make sure she was well away from Christian.
        Karl didn't go. He'd phone though.
        'For starters, Karl,' since I'd to trump him,
'even quiche takes a vacation.'
        Then I'm asked to 'Name your subjects, Soph.'
Since he's a lawyer too and wants to help.

The Course

        I had been living for my summer course
(what I expected would happen)
but Karl, who loved announcing
'Meet the Podes, quiche-masters to the Universe!'
Karl would soon be telling the obvious:
'Right now it's you and me, Soph.'
He was thirty, single, set on proving his way
as one of very few ways.
                It wasn't love
and there was too much of it.
I'd never liked him and here he was
getting me obsessed (if through my summer course).
        'All this,' Karl confessed
by the second week, 'brings out the bitch in you
and the bastard in me.'
             'Thanks,' I had to say.

Dealer

        There'd been an even simpler of proposals:
a friend of Karl's had hash-blocks, cheap.
He brought the dealer round.
                And the man's talk
was Rice Trail talk: Asia, drugs and women.
I bought the stuff and got him out.
        'So where'd you get your hideous friend?'
I asked to no reply except
        'Brings out Soph the schoolmarm does he?'
        'You're the one attempting show-and-tell,'
Karl was told.
        Which didn't faze him.

'Sophie, anyone can grow, sell to mates, share around...
but at *his* level nice guys needn't exactly deal.'

How did he know? Karl didn't.

I was hearing guesswork.

Oh yeah?

'Well he's no more my friend,' I'm told,
'than my accountant is.
You and everyone are so naïve.'

'But, I mean,
the Rice Trail, Karl?'

Then he turned hard:
'Does it alter the stone? If he had the slightest,
further notch of class, if he'd yabbered one word less,
if he wasn't some cabbie with this loud
Hawaiian shirt, you wouldn't have
that hash. In her head there's still the thrill,
that special Sophie thrill of slumming things.
So get that LLB of yours, and then defend him!'

Here's what happened every second evening:
Karl turned up, we argued, then got stoned
and fucked.

Why did I need so much of it?

Any of it?

The Case

It may mean little now
but remember the Kent case? I was five or six
when Dad became a national identity,
defending a cop-killer right to the gallows.

When I was seven or eight
he'd left the Bar and gone to the Corporation.

When I was eighteen we both had left
my mother; four years later Daryl was my husband
(everybody tolerated Daryl Pode) but Karl,
Karl Gold was my lover.

And other than rolling with Daryl into the gutter
the only worthwhile thing Karl seemed to do
for me was this: after I'd named
where my father worked and said I was sorry,

'Need you apologise?' Karl exploded.
'Since after what was done to him
(and you mustn't defend your Kents the way he did)
he had to work some place.'
      Soon Karl was even more enchanted
with the idea of Cross QC, telling me
'It was an election year,' as if that part of the legend
wasn't known. 'Hanging helped to keep
certain pricks in power. Your old man couldn't stand
the pace? Neither could I.'
              Had Karl read the case,
that Kent was a killer, total?
              Karl shrugged.
                    'Would you,'
I asked, 'give up all that you believed…for a killer?'
      The trick, he told me, was not to believe in
very much at all, which is what an activist,
his kind of activist, did.
      Sure I'd have taken him to Dad except
Dad was rarely in Melbourne now,
and Karl was not my husband.

Wife-man

      When I inform him
'You never listen much to women, do you?'
Karl tells me he hasn't done much else.
      When all of them are married how couldn't he,
being a wife-man: 'If you're a wife then I'm
your man.'
      We are in bed.
He rolls me onto my stomach.
And I'm saying what I have to say:
'Just a little gentler, Karl. Make it better
than last time. Love us a bit.'

Wife-man (continued)

Then Karl starts crying, actually crying,
knowing he is making it a mystery and how,
for me, all mysteries are made for solving;
so he tells me about the last wife
(how the husband was like Daryl, not a friend, really)
and how it never worked the way
it's working now.

Great-and-ratshit

It was the summer
everyone discovered some deadshit 'using'.
At a friend's place I saw a letter lying about.
'I'm using again...' the letter started.
But my time wasn't deadshit time.
I would have two months of summer course
overlaid with half as much again of Karl.
When they returned, Daryl and the household,
we held our biggest party,
where Karl kept calling him 'Dazza'.
Adrian arrived, took up with
a toke or ten and ran off with the nurse.
When he was gone a week his club,
keeping it out of the press, nearly sacked him.
That year the media would re-name him
'Mr Magic': meaning great-and-ratshit together,
since they were the words he used about the nurse,
needing to feel good about himself.
Like I do.
With Daryl home I am hating Karl.
Yet when he arrives I still follow him:
all over our big house.
My husband's taunted.
My husband doesn't know he's being taunted.
Karl asks 'Hey Commander, still slavin' over
the hot quiche?'
Daryl asks me
'What's wrong Soph?'

I can't stand the wimpery
passing for a spouse, and confess.

Gutter

Words are going to help, words like
It only happened twice, I was lonely,
Karl was helping me, he's hardly our friend,
it couldn't happen again.
                    Words until
one autumn afternoon in our front yard
he's out-staring Karl.
                    But it's only when
Karl advises 'Ah! Ah! Hold firm Commander Quiche!
Hold firm!' my husband jumps him.
From our path out they wrestle
into the road, then back to the gutter,
where Karl bites Daryl.

Grandma

Daryl, delighting in his ignorance,
embarrasses me.
                    When a household member
puts on some Bessie Smith
my husband hasn't got the brains or taste
to wait and find out who she was.
For him a name's enough.
                    'Who's that,' he giggles, 'Patti Smith's grandma?'
He's the grandma.
                    The household's
sighing hard.
                    Leave him!

Deal

'Go on,' Karl had dared,
'find out what it's like: get yourself a dealer
and defend him.'
                    And in a year
I may've had a degree in Law, but this career
in a damn lot less. Defence? Not quite.
I just worked for someone defending the best.
        And when I went out to Remand
no use in asking *Okay, just don't tell me
about it, right?* This one was going to anyway,
right?
        I flogged the Grange Hermitage of grass
once. Dealer? Now I merely work for one...'
and he'll also tell me:
'Them narcs hunting their movers 'n' shakers,
all they get's us shufflers 'n' wobblers...'
        He's the big boy of some small-town
carpet salesman for whom
'The present seems fairly dumb...' but yeah
you should've seen his dumber past.
        And then he adds:
'Except maybe most cops/all cops, someone
has to do it. And Sophie, that's my motto:
the dealers deal, the judges judge, that guy who draws
the funnies keeps drawing them. Even your old man
must do whatever he does...'
                            And now he'll say:
'Not me now but not horse.'

The Bench

        He was dreadful. (Can't anyone see how dreadful?)
So this is what happened: sent out to Pentridge
I'm to meet him, right? Kevin, sullen yet cocky,
innocent till proven, and he may have his past
but Kevin needs a chance and wants to prove
that chance; the interview room is chilly yet
his jacket comes off; he's laying it on the bench.

Nothing but Thunder

for Steve Anker

Could great men thunder
As Jove himself does, Jove would ne'er be quiet,
For every pelting, petty officer
Would use his heaven for thunder;
Nothing but thunder!

William Shakespeare *Measure for Measure*

But the best

of all is heroin. One day.
One day you'll own a big house.

John Forbes *Drugs*

But you've always had that touch of the flirt, eh Chrissie?
Bet you have.
Bet there never was a time you
weren't one. So, that's settled. Why kiss me? Why try?
Just to prove things? We're quite at ease right here:
you've got Kim, I'll have Soph and we can defer
any of your adolescent thrills.
Yeah? Me, I'm happy wondering
what exactly were those pills before the last lot,
since tonight it all seems clearer than it ever was.
Notice how I'm saying words I've heard and known
but hardly ever used? You might. Till then let's make that
lesson one on me: it's as if the pills supply a fuse
set on burning back. And strange how soon, you take
an afternoon for some, people find vacation friends,
and being Kim's girl now, well makes you one of us.
Besides, I said these pills keep fusing back: like a bomb
marked *confession* lying under my mind, say in some cartoon,
set to explode. And all tonight's that clear.
Y'know,
wasn't the sunset gross, almost chemical?
I glowed naked, sweat teeming away in the dusk.

After a shower I dressed, and standing on my balcony
glanced at the floodlit pool, saw nothing.
                                                Dreams stopped.
'Boss!' One of the wogs looked up waving. 'Hey,
Mister Kevin Joy!' Or whatever name I'd given the resort.
He pointed out this bar, just stood there grinning,
waiting his reward: a squat pharmaceutical tube
with a tip inside. 'Mister Kev, you still number one!'
and the night heard 'Thank you, thank you, thank you...' till
as it ended, I turned inside, gulped another
and descended.
                        Anxious? Sure I chewed a nail yet really,
feeling fine. Kimbo was smiling, he'd you at the bar, like
Look at this one here, Kev. We laughed you laughed,
all was A-one. The wog band posed C-and-W,
their lightweight serenades turning even lighter, and our luck
was working well as ever. Up north, deals getting dealt,
he'd met this bonus: a friendly Aussie girl, and I saw you
rub his legs. Sex or just affection:
who'd even guess? Kimbo logs up lots of ladies,
so maybe discrimination's been at times erratic?
Some chicks don't know when it's quits? But
I see he likes you heaps and, if not for keeps
trust Uncle Kev, it's a help this end of the 'gemstone trade.'

        Oh, and hadn't you bounced over Asia for weeks,
pricks like pogo-sticks and mmmm, how'd you phrase it?
Only thirty once Kev...yes divorced...a teacher's aide...
The tropics, liquor, dope and cocks, how potent Chrissie and
if you've spent time with other guys haven't these days
with Kim turned real trumps? If his hair recedes,
the teeth cave-in, he slumps, so what? What's required
he gives, what's lent gets returned. You'd months ticking
barbarian after dull barbarian off the list since
your divorce, and now we see that heady spacey calm
just being with him entails.
                                        I did. What was it
without Kim? Peddling leaf-in-foil to kids.
        Woman I lived with dabbled but, and that's important.
Which turned to use, that's important too, any extra cash
just pumped away. Droughts were even worse:

stoned-out on tequila for Chrissake,
and you could ask *Why bother with this useless bitch*
who just shoots up, making some rich Jew-boy richer?
You could ask that, I did. So we visited her dealer,
me and a mate, and soon I'm meeting Kim.

How'd I meet Soph?
You simply trust that jokers you have never known
can get you bailed, how if others fail the Morgans
can succeed. There's no choice, the fucker has to.
Funny sort of trust: I don't know anyone and my cash
just floats away. I'm Santa Claus!

So trust him? Yes,
for this was no case where the judge either snores or
doodles in the dust, the jury plays at gropies.
This could only be my stripes, my diploma, my three-gong award
Jeez you looked a goner, Kev. Sorry, wrong guy
and a whole damn planet set to split apart.

'You seem...' and Morgan's voice flowed forth sleek,
par for the job, 'a loner Kevin? I am not mistaken?'

Correct. He knew I couldn't beat him, had to join him.

Want to meet him? I can give one
unforgettable reference. Dirt? There'll be no dirt.
When Chrissie's sober we've a nice girl, she
only wants to flirt, only wants to suffer nights
like this and men like me for cash and Kim
and what would she love more?

Morgan loved his tones:
just relished teasing me to tough it:
he knew who suffered: 'Won't defend dealers
Mr Joy. Addicts, sure. Understand?' We'd read
the papers. We knew. Knew how any shit-heap of ideals
tapers away the more you're offered. Four yachts now
float with his name.

As Kim now floats with yours.
No use pining for some half-stoned teacher
you've divorced, or bothering with the ocker hoards
of Asia. You needed someone, enter Kim and all
the smorgasbord reduced itself to this:
either make it *now!* or just break off before it
even starts. Which won't work. What beats the might

of what you want? And nothing feels better than
a night of *Gimme gimme take it take it* right
past a tropical dawn.

But think of a chilled, wet
annex in Remand. The least it needed was manners:
I took my jacket off, laid it on the bench.

'Who's this?'
she blinked. But you give what you can
in such a place. 'Thanks…I'm Sophie Cross.
I'm with your solicitors…' Piling on the fidgets,
apprehensive, perhaps scared, and I know she caught
the damp stench they tried to excuse as plumbing.
Supposed to be October. I shrugged as this
slow, cracked heater tried numbing the room.
Had to talk, clear the muggy tension.
What's the tale, Kevin, why you here?

'…I've liked people, that's not clever. This time?
Trusting the wrong bastards. Remember,'
she got informed, 'I'm needing help and that is what
you give Miss Cross, why I hire you lot.
Lectures are for the cops and then I don't listen.
You listen. I've sold grass before, who hasn't,
it's not me now but. Not horse. Y'smoked dope?'
She had and sweat grew a damp fuzz over
her top lip. 'Well this is different, Sophie. Not in it.
Never.'

Were we playing? She thought I was.
I thought she thought I was. She thought I thought
she thought I was and yet, name any more
appropriate game, or better one, for a first time.
Guess we were scared, Soph with her class
and me my class-of-a-kind (class enough to risk
and make her mine when later I'd be hers.
We hadn't even touched.) With narcs mad for my scalp,
remember we're just smaller stuff, I needed anyone,
just like some dag botting smokes outside a third-
rate youth club dance. Why sacrifice a swell
organisation poised to roll, for just a few
questionable grams, two junkies drying out
and fate? Next time I gave my hand, we shook,

not scared now, nervous but, and fifteen years in the can
apart, my case seemed almost passé. But then
our routine was stopping all the *I employ/you work*
it never had. Her hands were moist. Each day
till she arrived I'd get headaches added to wanting her,
needing to want her, for Chrissie, just
to count her mine would complete me!

                                        Yeah?
But who'd ever blunder in to loving Kevin Joy?
And why risk giving myself those daily/nightly
friskings of doubt? Sweet bitch bound me in options.
I was Sophie-crazed by now sure, but
was it even worthwhile showing this?
Talk of hedging your bets, then, cadging
one of her Kents she touched my arm.
'Don't fret.'

               Oh yeah?

                      'Don't fret Kevin. He's a whiz...'
She snapped into work whilst I stared out
twitching like a lizard.

                              Those places make you imagine.
Shaving, like, I'd catch my Joy Boys file round me
for the group shot. Or, awake by three I'd lie there
whilst the sun got nearer, gibbering:
What happens when everyone left in the mirror goes
and I'm the only broker? And get up pale,
poker-faced, a headache growing, advising
Kevin, don't doubt it, this games beyond even love
or money, without it you might as well be some
joker running his used car yard. Not any clown imports!

            I'd never felt this deliberate, I needed a pause
to borrow hours that wouldn't be her. An affair?
Couldn't that brim me up with fears, kill me
risking it? Like you Sophie's a good girl.
Good girls fuck the best. They love it. For keeps.

            And tonight all my will we/ won't we
lies resolved. She flies in tomorrow.

                                   Want to deal?
Simple. Go to any Hicksville, ask round for a drinking mate,
but ask quietly, only dags are caught and you

want to be found!

        Had a *Playboy* once:
you imagine this stir: thought I'd make some friends,
be a two-bob-a-peek entrepreneur. You can't.
There's a boy pushing smut! Cops got told
and the school pumped out its giant taskforce.
Dumb buggers, dumber Kevin, they were after
freebees! Whole town wanted to blow! Me?
I just smiled back: what's that?
If you have something they need, you work.
Not easy, dealing, just simple. And stunts
which end, end. That night saw me peeling page
after page, watching them flap into the ocean.
Bye-bye Miss March 1963, you'd keep,
somewhere. I wasn't set for any slanging match.
Like, on any rock group's North Coast tour I'd hang
outside the youth club dance with all those other dags.
Well? Who needs the collective will
of a few hundred fat virgins caked in Clearasil?
We weren't known and wanted nothing.
Take any Sydney street, who'd notice me?
That's an easy salvation dags learn well:
the anonymous pull the best stunts. Sometimes.

        We learn but. All my old man did was nod.
I opened the door and sat beside him.

        'You're an idiot, Kevin,' and Howard drove on
through the streets of Lawrence muttering.

        I saw a smart-arse wave. *Piss off* I blushed. Some kid
whose dad we knew, who then turned into every prick
in town. We both squirmed. All the red-hot respect
that Howard craved puffed-off in embarrassment:
knew the Headmaster from Lodge, see.

                     And 'Kevin Joy,'
this toad announced, 'wants to say a few words
to the assembly.'

        But then he had to. Sorry, school,
won't happen again. Nup. Not bad for a dag.
Pretending to be something out of Carter Brown
we'd wagged it see, brought a girl back for something
planned if unspecified, till the stupid Head arrives and

'Sorry Sir, it's me mates, they've locked her in this wardrobe...'
        Well I surprised them, see. Apologies become me,
all things do when needed.
                           But he won't hurry, why should he?
The boy who has to say sorry gets called to the dais,
rising to crown himself King of the Dags. And he doesn't
stand before Lawrence High School now but this:
a champagne march past, magnum after magnum,
whilst slater bugs, the norm, kids in uniform
stare up.
        I left that year, not knowing how
I'd seen the future, what would be mine:
house, boat, houseboat, car, girls, Sophie and champagne
nobody drank but me. Then though I'd only one ambition:
to quietly state *No, never fuckin' again.* What else?
Marry, hit the piss and attempt another generation
of carpet salesmen? A mate 'n' me left and Lawrence
never got a chance to cry *Poooor buuggah!* Chrissie,
you try kissing any hometown bye-byes with this
block of farts...nearly died with the pleasure.
                               Why look
so pained? Tampon packets might lie strewn through
your place: such bravado hides nothing. Aren't we
so respectable? Wanting to slum it? Expect
the barest manners. Can't tell why I'm talking still
except those pills perhaps, except you're heading paralytic,
have great little tits and, given a day or two
these raves can end, this tourist junk you wear
will get replaced. We're used to sprucing girls as
stenographer, nursing sister, teacher's aide. But yet
it's more than *used*, all of us love the gall, daring
and that warm cash coming back home, just to roost
on respect. We disappoint no-one. We serve all clients,
often before ourselves, with a market so delighted
to love us, have us love them. If say I owned
Carlton and United I'd be Sir Kev. Great but shove it,
for Chrissie where would be the love? And what is it?
Why to know you love *is* love, and better,
to know that you can reach for more than just the lot.
I'm not another bearded teacher *just cultivating*

backyard stuff who freaks each time a chopper flaps
above him.
              See, everything was turning special:
I was getting this place up north, a wide, white,
isolated monster being carved out of a headland
you had to arrive by tunnel. I needed to think
the how and what and who to fill it. For the show
was moving: contradictions, fabrications Morgan proved
just that, simple disappearances. Time then
for all those remaining Joy charms to get reactivated.
How I loved 'n' hated it, laughed when found out giving
'So, where you living, Sophie?' for a line.
                                        'Me?'
she responded.
              Yeah you and no-one else.
         'I'm never at home,' and Sophie smiled
'get me at work. South Yarra. My apartment...'
         All choices narrowed, we heard the other breathing;
give me a week I'd visit her.
         'Not guilty.' The foreman marked it plain,
plain as Sophie gasping 'Kevin, we won!'
She couldn't embarrass me, here was the girl I wanted.
You can't love *that* much and me I only love winners.
So, like beginners again we were stalking ourselves.
In less than a week but quicker and quicker
I'd shed my cover of cool, totting up grass, perfume, dinners,
whatever she'd want: clothing, trips to Paris.
         And couldn't I feel the rest, what shot up my spine
and down, as over in a hotel's plushest suite
the Boys would see our party on track. Me, I needed to pause,
for Chrissake all risks had been mine and always were.
How could this Sophie woman even attempt being
capital B bad? Oh she'd see it that way and yes
she'd love to try, but how could her reputation
ever bruise except that it'd be mine? The world
believes nice girls, they have nothing to lose.
Could I believe enough to stake myself with her,
with Sophie?
              Jim is propping by this mound of oyster shells
scooping caviar whilst all our party eyes us, her and me.

'So?' says Jim. 'It's their fix…'
They get nix, 'cause that night nothing scared me
more, you know, than her: Morgan patting the ringlets
like she was his pup. You'd all keep: we tried them,
they'd tried us. They delivered, we delivered. Below,
another town, a market, relaxed. Nothing at all
was wrong and this was class. A tax adviser
had to leave, '…great party Kev…' '…take care matey…'
Vast ranks of them would hurtle on down
if someone really probed, or say tried to begin it.
How come? There is no 'crime' and we are partners in it.

       Three well-known merchant bankers get farewelled,
then Kim sidles up with cigars. 'That lawyer-bird,'
he murmurs, 'she's got you on the brain.'

       Ho ho, funny place for a brain but right, 'cause she
looked at me then laughed as if *Oh, oh, shot you Kevin Joy
bang! with my round dark eyes!* Well well surprise surprise:
wasn't it time to get ambushed by class?

       Not quite yet. Morgan stood aside, munching party pies
as Kim bragged: 'Wasn't I correct? He's like you Kev,
the best.'

       Reputations never did harm:
X slaps on the charm, Y splats the prosecution
like it's sumo, Z snow-jobs the juries;
and as with some tart whose talent's in blow-jobs
you pay for the mouth.

       Oh I'd been calm,
till the verdict, but then I needed to cut everything,
almost wanting to sweet-talk any narc. Go on why not?
What's the Chrissie line: Kevin Joy sucks? Haven't I,
courtesy of a judge and jury the greatest of credentials
Not guilty? Yet dazed (and almost near-amazed
by my remaining market) I'd left the court to be alone.
(We're raking it off the surface, there's *that much*
Chrissie, and sometimes even *that much* can wait.)
Real making it starting tomorrow, I erased yesterday
strolled into Henry Bucks, ordered a suit.

       Jim snapped me with this Dom Perignon:
'Smile you happy bastard smile…' I couldn't, I was unnerved
that night, needing someone, anyone, to keep Soph occupied,

or else I'd simply slide on in and it would be it.
      Hold on but: 'Hey señor you fuckin' marvel!'
My brother Basil offered her boss a toke, but neither smoke,
and so he giggled something like:
'Planning to toss the odd run too. Keep you on side?'
and later: 'So we've cooked up beeg money, señor?'
But Basil's always excused, I would anyone approaching
blood, kin, relations, whatever way you tag it,
providing they don't grass, 'cause even if he's an alkie,
no doubt a faggot (you'd hate him) Basil's jibber-jabber
is open slather on deadshits. It's Daffy Duck
for a brother, all another language, he's my real, live
deadshit detector, right? Why'd I want more?
I don't because he won't be bought. 'You find this,'
he scoffed to Morgan, 'worthwhile? Look, look
who's king of the shit-heap: me brother Kev. On yer, Kev!'
I watched Morgan sipping, staying his balance, smirking
through all the piss Basil held and 'Bud-deeee!'
the endless Black-power salutes, as if *Ho ho young man…*
Well ho ho Morgan, lick the nipper's boots, even the odd
flock of vultures got to sell themselves, even dags
want somehow to be checked over, vetted and accepted,
just clean enough to cop all those predictable hints.
      I don't get blasé, mind. I open my eyes real wide
to suck the info in *Huh? Y'don't say? Really mate?*
Taa. Won't forget it. Aren't there times it's best
to bite the lip, nod and catch the advice they palm
across? Of course it's best like *Next time obey*
the eleventh commandment Kev: don't get caught. Weren't they
there to amuse, help me pronounce the champagne brands?
      For the party turned to this glorious shunting yard:
anyone of use on either dope or a retainer,
my dreams, proposals, orders turning themselves to the truth,
this wad of lawyers soaking up the dregs they lived off,
loving it, for just one night never getting enough of Kevin Joy and
the Joy Boys: voyeurs over a life they needn't explain or,
after their tolerance leached into tomorrow morning,
not have to concern them again.
                        But not Soph.
I hadn't been so sliced-to-pieces as when her body brushed

that ever-so-slightly by, wrapping me round in chills,
hoping tonight he couldn't imagine such the sweetest bitch
in creation murmur him aside like
Y'great, Kevin. Let's meet again? Please?
Till, as its tide could hardly consider stopping,
love would sink them into its glitzed forever.
Love ? Oh Kev-in, only sucks contemplate that
in the script. Keep telling yourself no matter how
top shelf this one is, she's potent. Keep your trousers zipped,
all the available steps between you both were danced
in Remand. You'll chance what for what?
Wardrobes of snappy businesswomen's suits can't fool me,
she's crazy, ten times fuckin' wilder than you ever were.

       Then, a few days on, I glanced through a phone book:
found I was just waiting to con myself.
It named this smallish block of flats I thought
I recognized. Sweet small events had blown my cover,
those odd beautiful occasions.
In court, say, she writes him notes. Notes?
For Kev that's bullion from the tip. *Find better,*
God or the world got ordered, and they didn't, didn't because
she cared, I flipped and the future was on,
even the present was over.

       He's catching his cab in a heatwave,
this man with an enormous bouquet of roses.
What more is needed to snap *pffft!* at the past
since someone helped, the foyer was unchecked;
must've ignored any intercom and can't recall any
lift-ride up, only those few seconds outside her door
were spent feeling my heart pummel each rule
of organisation I'd ever set. But she was different, I knew it:
almost fearing (and yet near daring) her to package me
prime-cut, blue-ribbon, take-me-back-to-your-mother.

       Who or what taught Miss Sophie Cross to blush, recover
and coo 'Roses...aren't *you* a darling...'
Camberwell Church of England Girls Grammar School?
How long was I to be sent mad-and-a-half just wanting
to kneel, tongue her clit, see what followed,
as if I wasn't aware, hearing how Soph was
'Crazy for you Kevin.' Still, there was time to think

Like how does class, real class screw? With heartbeats
refusing to take up her slack and Soph at her bathroom
saying like how she'd be back (and now I know that sweet routine
by rote) then smiling she returned, split and I entered
for we were, and Chrissie you got to hear this,
lovemakers...lovemakers nothing less.
And more: getting told how much she missed me
that unhinged enough, turned me too mute to reply,
but I knew then, if other women existed, I was tamed
if ever Sophie said so, making me feel, well
ashamed if you like, I'd contemplated Rent-a-Root back
in Remand. Tarts bored me. That week, concealing little,
those dogs, the Joy Birds got the shove-along;
with one real lady-lady ripening for the rage, you think
I'd ever page Dial-a-Date just to sop that extra cash
I'd gotten around to spend?
Don't shit me! Don't play me further games of let's pretend,
please use a few brains and imagine Chrissie how we were
blessed by the gods of love, Cupid and his gang!

      Oh he exists. I saw him tonight. That wog
who signalled Kim's return, for love, dope, cash and friends,
there's little between them. A god, a wog?
I was satisfied. He made me happy as Kim can,
you could, and as always Soph wraps me in,
get this one...joy! If fucking alone were love,
and even I've gotten round to learning it isn't,
but imagine if it was, we'd always want to double-the-lot,
being so wired to get-get-getting.
No wonder sucks need more, no wonder they still fall
for stunts like that stupid mock-mock flirting
you've been doing since we met.
Just by wanting it love can be smack.
Don't I know what the world needs now, Mister Bacharach!
People want and I'm their kind of Cupid. What wouldn't begin
were I to have Kaiser Stuhl, Carlton and United,
the Dom Perignon stunt? *Arise, Sir Kev, gobble your oysters,*
keep those pearls, unfurl your coat of arms and my!
what a smart silk shirt and matching tie you're sporting.
But since Kimbo and me and yes you now are importing
love first and profit only later, I tell you

that makes for real danger. And they're frightened.

       Like I was. This could be love, real love. I knew it,
could never demand it. Orders were over and minus them
what was I? Soph had to tell quick:
some crim to notch up for a whim,
or the one man to scream for: imagine the narcs, say,
bursting in halfway through screwing *I'm his lawyer:*
what in the hell y' think y' doing? Giving her all for him
him him and that him me! Could it be that?
Oh understand how someone really loved me,
Kev the dag, and it was to be all dreams, if only
for a night: when even deals and cash could never
drag me awake. And better than dreams were her eyes,
eyes that screamed out *Yes Kevin yes!*
and would you believe maybe I was horrified?
As if whatever gods were operating knew
even *I* cried for someone, and had set me with a lady
brave or crazed enough to chuck her lot,
like only good girls can when they're in love.

       Like Chrissie will for Kim, not of course
for some manic dag she thinks is sitting opposite. I've
caught onto that, but you, you were waved-on hours back:
it's been like talking to my legs (when you're sober
you might get that one) *Hello legs, quite soon*
you'll stroll through Customs be climbing into a cab...
But hasn't the drum been given now how many times?
Point one: even if you've got a headache, bursting to piss,
relax. I've said the facts: what narcs, cops and judges
are with us. How many? About the world at times,
although I'm middling. Funny how I don't own a freight
terminal, a trucking firm. The Joy Boys big?
We're big enough to buy off those who think we are.
Just middling but: I'm no corporate bastard,
not for *them* that tense, crazed delight
of a crushing. They've football teams to buy,
chat shows to appear on. Why bother skiting over
some arse of a journo you had slugged,
even sacked, or who's been tagged your 'judge of the month'?
Know these men Chrissie real men?
Real men never see the stuff.

Like: what's this heroin really like then?
Something in bags on the Six o'clock news...
and their grandkids will be moving Ks by laser beams.

But Jim was anxious. Sophie was excessive. It wasn't
that he'd never mixed with class, he never wanted to.
Old Kimbo you can guess just lay down and floated
into her charm: 'Kev's lawyer-bird's an asset,
makes him almost respectable.' Not our dumb Jim but.
Didn't want to see. Poor shrink who tries frisking
your skull. What's this overweight Tongan without me?
'Look here Jungle Jim,' he's told, 'she's hardly a risk,
she's not on smack, she's a lawyer get it?
Stick to the gee-gees, you're backing the wrong 'un this time.'
Had to be kept on but, for propping my Boys are always legmen,
gamblers. He bores me? But the whole game
almost can and I was stale enough at times to vow
retirement, tomorrow. Tomorrow sure, the next time.

Out on the tan track my head was swampy with ideas,
gelling slowly into schemes. Next time sure.
But Soph 'n' me changed gears: relaxing into parties,
wine, coke, sleep and each other.

One Saturday
she drove me to her old school fair, my tête-a-tête
with class. Class? Couldn't I buy out the lot? And spent
a second, even less, seeing my retirement. One more run say?
Imagine: wiping the frigging slate...to what?
There must be a next deal and a next. That's all.
Why join those mutts just wanting to exist? I need
to live, to feel myself curl round and into every
part of fate.

Men (her friends? husbands of her friends?)
approached, trying to hold the booze through lunch.
I clutched my plastic cup, tried looking I belonged
to whatever they were, even if my skull was gonged
with headaches. Of course I stayed:
you choose to stay with Sophie Cross, parade her arm
through yours. Spuds with sour cream,
lamb on a spit, wog food, who wouldn't send
their kids to such a place?

'Coming back?'

One of her brothers (was it?) drove me, dealing facts:
some famous quack lived here…the Minister for that
lives there, pleased, he poked the air, men like him
want things like that known. *When you following Soph?*
Without you I've this flair for s.f.a., and I stood,
blank as any Asian, helping this brother bury me
in small talk: 'Meet Kevin. With him a spade's
a regular spade.'

          'Hi, he thinks I'm direct…'
Know what I do fellas? '…mainly gemstones, bits
of developing…'

          Hands lay resting over my shoulders:
'Always our shout here, Kevin, what'll it be?'

          Rich kids, lucky kids on smack making suckers
of the folks?

          Don't wince, clever Chrissie made a guess,
next clever Chrissie makes her run, a few days pass, their luck,
her luck, our luck's notched up again,
best game in town: once it hits the blood it
and all that's bad just vanishes.

          No, that day it wasn't hard
being a dag, one more anonymous rich dag.
Not enough gel for a stockbroker but all right,
this skinny, tanned joker with crazy, grey-blue
Paul Newman eyes, he'll do. He sleeps, shits, eats
and sleeps again. Never seen a living thing that
won't die. Something will start in space, and we'll turn
as cold 'n' dry as Mars. But don't get told different:
I'll even love her beyond Pluto. *Heard about this crim
and his nice girl, fellas?* Get this: after Soph suggested
I insure my prick with Lloyds, she stripped and I
covered her in fifties, took polaroids. *Like to see
some snaps, fellas?*

          They let me hang in there. *Kevin?
Seems a quiet type.* Not much to say, that's why;
until her little sister, wanting a crack of the Joy magic,
starts to flirt. You know what's best, girl? Go wait
in your folks' laundry, we won't leave 'til the place
tastes almost too thick of steam, detergent, us and cash,
your address book packed, praying to get smacked.

Who knows what any kid sister does, given enough
of what she wants and promised more? True, not anyone
can pull these stunts, and hijacked by headaches
I couldn't, that day. Wouldn't you rather dreams?
Dreams that are working or dreams that have even
arrived?

But then give *you* five minutes, say,
and isn't Chrissie's one-time husband always re-occurring?
Ray always says…Aren't former fucks a near professional
obsession? Or present ones since I should talk.
Well just like you I too can wince, wince at the mention of
Ray's mighty sense of humour for the tenth time.

Later, with Kimbo off to bed, the flirting getting nowhere,
Our bar lining up another round, and no you didn't need them mixed,
neat was enough…later it's Ray this Ray that
screaming for all the room, 'How dare you think I'm drunk!'
No, if you say so, and once again your marriage gets recycled.
Ray's history, there's only Kim now sweetheart.
Know why you're joining him? We've money, love, the future.
Pension off the past, why remain there? When whacked
do you always mention this Ray, this genius Dylan-freak teacher?
Fed-up being someone's ex, with a life of bit parts?
We've an upcoming feature starring, simply, you.
Any Joy Bird will vouch how its easy bringing a case
to Customs, bracing yourself just as the Valium allows.
Relax. On Two-grand-plus a month that underwear-
shuffling narc is one of ours. Near the city this friend
will pace a flat. His phone rings, pacing ends for the day,
with each question answering itself: *yes!*
Our game's on hold, the pack has been shuffled and cut,
the dice are poised to roll, he hangs up and the call
unfolds like some huge and magic cum:
the deaf hear, the dumb speak, on, on, just like a religion,
miracles et cetera, person after person happier and happier.

And aren't you pleading till you're numb with this
I've been respectable, I'm still nice? Anyone is
if that's how they want it. Nobody's nicer, scout's honour.
Though here, up north things are different. Simple. On a visit
you met someone to amaze your friends: yourself.
Asia provides all a nice girl needs to escape caddying

for genius egos, to fend off sugar-daddying.
As Chrissie bummed Thailand, Malaysia with Kimbo
all her answers bloomed: you're a goner for thrills,
forever primed to blossom out in shudders. You didn't exclaim
Drugs eh? That'll be a buzz! You merely looked it
and why not? Tonight all covers floated off,
that's easy when we're both stoned-drunk, short of keeling
to the floor of course of course, you're not that pissed.
Kev's a ready bunny, Chrissie wants his ear, any ear.
Still worried over all that cash owed to your sainted Ray?
Just wait, smack kills off any debt, magic always does,
or love if there's enough of it.
                             But listen!
What's that? Beyond the wog band packing their gear,
those few remaining couples chatting-up. What?
No need to wonder. Nothing but thunder. Just that. Listen
and imagine even if our dusk had sent its own storm-warning
ever felt safer? Couldn't you drink on through till dawn
to view the resort blundering back for breakfast?
I'll let you upstairs soon, want to stay raving but?
Let's pretend we can tell anything, let's say you're some
lady cop. I'd buy you.
                      There but. That noise again. Thunder!
Almost a friend now. And you might imagine galaxies where that's
a warning…not in mine: it's an order, lightning follows:
and since you or anyone can be as bought as smack
(or thunder) can't I calculate the where, when, how and why
of anybody?
                    Let me tell you how The Human started
bloating till he rose. Some fucker hadn't weighed him down,
gasses grew and up he bobbed, floating the Harbour
like shit. Grassing moves both ways:
Harper, this cop I knew, traced Operation Overdrive
to him. I survive by juggling payments, attempting
to keep the remainder tidy. Why just exist but?
I had to thrive and The Human needed to go.
It all freaked me, weren't we kind of friends? Yes
but hardly colleagues. What was he? A pest. Why?
Because stuffing it he had to grass.
                    Anything's a drug: a run, a hit, a kill. Life by nerve-ends:

after that first you may never want to try another
but all the rest get easier. Guess what?
We're just doing a job and nothing happens.
Facts stick, if indeed they're facts, only if you're careless.
Who'd want that? You can get more 'n' more.
Something is to be done? You'll do it. Like facts
your first run just happens. It's no huge step
taking on this. You're protected. The right people know,
know I'm very generous that, like tonight, the night before
and the night before, any night's on me.

                                    Soph but,
she's different, let's talk of Soph then. No? Kimbo? Later?
If our guest wants...same for the lady, waiter.
Huh? Don't call you *that*? Don't call you *lady*? Oh well,
blame the pills, blame whatever Chrissie's latest little fad is.
And don't you want to be so extra-good?
Though why must your confessions keep on with
their same reminders: *Ray's got himself a little lady...*
Michelle 'n' I we really get on. Woman where you from?
Just couldn't believe hearing *Anyway, what's money?*
The reason you're trying to con me to accept *I'm this hippy,*
well kinda.

                        Maybe cash is shit, you've still needed it.
Needed to let Ray bail you out the times
you're going broke. I know the score: girl drinks,
still cannot forget him, screaming at the bar boohoo,
boohoo, you'd clutch at anything, clutch like
Ray's got himself a little lady now. She a dwarf?

                        Don't pout. Only trying to joke. You'll know if I'm not.
                        The Human didn't. Talking about him wasn't I?
Had to leave, going to dob us, cops poised to once more
bust him. Like who'd ever trust him?
He'd been big, fat-gutted slime, always picking up the tab
to buy some friends. He used and that's important
since he was a wreck, though it never depended on junk but,
the excuse was him, it's just about everyone's.
Shrinks try weaving us into something they think
is just this little bit unique: fat chance.
So here's Harper barging in at four a.m. bust-style:
'Human's floating. What fucker did you hire? Stay sweet.

Without me Kevin you'd be floating too...'
Pleasant bloke Harper. Though he can't get out any more
than Chrissie can. And it's this simple:
why would he leave us and why would you?
Still wondering where that famous buck stops? It doesn't.
Nobody's straight, it's only their price hasn't been
arrived at. It always will. With cops, junkies,
we only know one dance. Like I said fat chance.

     Who hated The Human? Half Sydney. The other lay
indifferent, covered in two words *Drop it.*
But for a day I went walking, just that, ground into
a half-trance. Why were we that thick? How?
Harper got his slice and I got out.

     Back in Melbourne, uncertain, not enough of a local.
So? I knew of another tale: once upon a time see,
there's this North Coast yokel, hits Sydney
becomes a legend. Needs to stop just grassing safe-jobs, see.
Meets Kimbo. And next, you could almost plan,
within a year this young guy's receiving how-many-Grand
a month, watching respect and self-respect grow with every deal.

     He's back in Melbourne but. Stuck with the biggest but;
grassing. Like Jasmin 'n' Mick, two friends a.k.a.
Lara 'n' Max, nice folks real nice folks
were passing lies for facts, for cash, for dope.
Shame: whatever names they'd given. Either them lifting the lid,
or Patty the Courier Kid, out of school and whoosh!
straight on the game.

     And now there's someone interstate
whose help I need: today, not tomorrow
and I'd prefer last week. We'll call him Bill.
Ninety Grand straight to your account, Bill, c.o.d. each cassette.
Of course we suspected them, Jaz 'n' Mick but jeez,
put it this way, ever hear yourself being bad-mouthed to the narcs?
The mouth dries, the guts drop and Chrissie, that's what people are,
. you've always known it. They'd blown it, sure, but all
their bad-mouthing and lies turned them to shark bait
when it stopped. Not even bait now.

     'This about does us, eh Kev?' as he curled
onto her. Tough luck, Mick. Checkmate, mate.
Look, he never tried acting the hero and I admire it,

admire their drying-off programs, stuffing down the 'done.
You ever put a feeler out for smack? Please don't.
It's nothing, a real nothing.
(I liked them once, they weren't using then.)
Try losing yourself on something Chrissie can control,
Kimbo say. (For when the end arrived they hadn't.
Having no Kim they just glittered for a while.)
       Or I'll say what I said to Lisa:
'There might be excitement, sure. Try forgetting it.
The glam's peripheral. Our world is bordered by
one word: organisation. Have I to slam each syllable
till it sticks? *Look they're nar-cot-ics. Ill-e-gal.*
I could love them like the inevitable garden parties
they're not, but they're not.'
                  Think after barking
long enough, something clicks? So what she just
wouldn't understand you must: without orders one more pinhead
rushes in, little's questioned, nothing's answered.
Like one more fad she's picked up from yet another client:
imitation battery cells, more bells than a cathedral.
'Please…' and you know how it goes, 'we'll have a great time…
love you Kev…please this once…' till, and imagine this,
she would do anything. You're game as Lisa, right?
Wanna drop Kev's strides, meet the Leaning Tower of Pisa, no?
' Course she could flinch like that: 'Not tonight.
Please mate. Headache. I want out…' Knew she did.
       And knew how, like her, the lot had always returned,
driven by just this: they needed to be in it.
Why give Lisa the benefit of some half cooked-up
conscience? If indeed it was? And yet
why bother snarling further orders, she lived in a free world.
Why mention just how small this free world was?
And some things were necessities for Lisa,
their steady beat held on, in any day she'd almost
break her neck or anyone's, just to return and help.
Lisa, I told you, would do anything.
So even, I thought, her judgement might be working, but
'Kev…this chick…something to snort?' Heh heh.
How'd I suspect? Within a week cops are attempting
to quiz me. Or like, she hadn't dreamt of a takeover,

had she? There'd been orders to check, cash was down
on Lisa now. And where is she? Somewhere, I think,
on forged papers. I've been told, I want to forget and
I mean to say how Lisa had her orders but Lisa wouldn't obey.
She flew but. Helped Morgan, Soph and me to stuff them.
     'So maybe,' Jim got told, 'the gods exist.
Haven't we beaten 'n' joined them?'
and as my breakfast lay just brimming
I knew I'd found enough of sweet sweet love to shout:
'I'm free, I've won, I've Soph...
and the whole bloody world is opening up!'
     Kimbo I telegraphed *fly down and celebrate*
I'm out and heading north.
     So, when I arrive he has you just like we've had so many,
comfy: one more yacht, another mortgage paid,
disappearing debts and since my freedom props so much
I'm needed out and needed total.
My generosity getting gorged as bait? Fine.
Who else could feed them, dress them my way.
Joy Birds should look just as Lisa looked:
so straight a narc might blush to think, no cop
would ever let her stop.
     We'll wipe your debts, keep you
a very comfy Chrissie, remember but my clear
and necessary orders. Better *know* them. And try,
please try not getting this pissed again. You can stand?
Let's go up. I've some Berocca in my suite.
You'll need them.

Leo

for Robert Langsford

I've a friend, guess this one's myself,
for effect though, please think he's a mate.
Any ambitions sir? Yes, to be a top shelf
cruiser, as if the earth might evaporate
tomorrow. A favourite memory? Hubbies puffing
homeward from a night-jog, an enjoyable task
done. He terms the business, not merely for nothing,
Free Entertainment in the Parks
(though what *they* may call it never escapes,
a pity). One evening on this *Hi-there!* famous beat,
stage right, two truckies. Maybe he'll traipse
off with the taller, but...
                              'We've others, like to meet
our mates?'
                 And I, or my friend (or was it his friend?)
...any way our hero blanches
as two, then another three arrive. Can't defend
himself. The trees would be as branches
and branches, twigs with these guys.
He can sprint, but if he made it
to his car there mightn't be time to...surprise!
'We only want some fun!' And they did:
fair dinkum fun. Just one thing
leading wherever one things head.
                              Their caution, if slight,
remained, each kept nit by rote, all had their something
to contribute though. He licked the late spring air, the night,
park and flowers had that much life!
For, with such a mass of willing beaux
to help what, at twenty-three, you want to try, try
and try again, seven at one blow
(as were) you better believe it! They had to be camp of course,
one or two maybe not. For seven 'normal' men
with just, you know, the need to horse-
round with themselves, no, not often just now 'n' then...
oh dear!

They tidied and headed to a flat,
he driving a boy who shrugged as if it was over,
it was nothing and, well, never done quite that. And *that*
was hard to accept.

Under a full moon's spooky cover
tenants were putting out their bins.

'Come in sport. Never know when there's a party.
Always keep y' fridge well stocked with tins.'

And, talking of work or whatever, till 'We like you matey,
but tell us...'

'Mmmm?'

'What's it like being a poofter?'
Our friend squinted, had to shrug (but not like the boy had).
'...please...we're interested.'

Wasn't the time to smash-off the roof or
improvise a lecture, or even to be mad
enough risking *You mean you don't know?* 'Life,' he mumbled.
'Suppose it's that. What's anything?'

And, as if it answered more than enough the boy stumbled
up to turn the tele on. They continued drinking
till the taller guy, who'd convened proceedings
somewhat finished them. 'We like you mate...serious.'

Like? You've loved me as you've never liked. Any pleadings
otherwise are shit. Seven blokes delirious
with their game drank on.

'I'm meeting a friend...'

'Yeh? Catch yer.'

With those two hour's bemusing fol-de-rol
never forgotten, he drove off. 'Music to Midnight' had Satchmo
playing and singing one of his best: *Body and Soul.*

from
The Great Australian
Songbook

Down Under

I.M. Richard Hall

The head still full o' zombie?

                         Yet on Orchard Rd
be honest, man! Your regulation Harry Lee short b and s
goes with the lightweight, straight-if-casual dress
sense you've acquired, helping to wean a three-month load
of what's smoked in those hills up north.

                             And, if here the law
is 'Fit in Western Freak', well a brain may yet take off
to one stoned night you tripped into their pigshit trough
but rose back grinning at the tribesmen; or that pleasing twelve-hour lockjaw
session and how 'With gear like *this*,' you mused,
'not merely fortunes but our souls are made!'

    So how?

                    Well, one mate's ex-in-law's this dodgy narc,
whilst another (he's fevered with the prospects!) reckons on someone who's
'Like something someplace in some gemstone trade...'

       'G'day,' you'll hear a sardonic Kiwi mutter, 'I'm Terry Clark.'

It's Time

for Don Sharp

      Democracy, face it, cannot be denied,
for I've shared my three hours at the how-to-votes
with this man round my age, from the other side,
and his arch, down pat, patent Young Lib quotes:
'Polls? Forget 'em! This'll be down to the wire...'
He nods, the eyes narrow, he strokes the jaw,
a silly prick who knows I'm holding fire
on Billy Bigears, conscription and the war.
      'But look...' I turn conciliator, 'we won't seize power
for...how many years? Twenty three?'
                          And he's nodding 'Yeah...'
(Both shifts have drifted to the concession hour.)
'I'll grant this much, you've got a great song there.
It's time! Why didn't we think of *that*?
Yeah...'
      But in *your* case it'd be time for...what?

On The Road To Gundagai

...heading straight for home
Jack O'Hagen

After church the drive, the singsong: Dad in tenor mode
winds the Vauxhall down Mount Dandenong Road;

lulled, Mum's glad, these patterns still keep:
Janet reading, Carol pulling faces, Margie asleep.

Till, beyond such certainties, each arrives
(stride-, stroll- or stumbling through their lives)

out of those soul-on-sleeve
days, with what was/ is/ might be something to believe.

So Dad dies, Mum re-marries and shifts,
Janet lectures, Carol designs, Margie drifts.

Oh millstone/ loadstar
(that time of faiths/ a Sunday in the car)

behold your future, its, by extension, splendour:
welcome, ladies to The Age of Gender!

The Never Never

This is as much about trust as truth.

Brisbane. A decade starts.

Brenda walks to school with Letty, one of the older girls.
Both grow up in a town that's still unfurled
as pioneer-genteel.

Which (nodding slowly to itself) soon departs
once they join the Army, my mother and a few of her friends:
*Yes there's a war yes we've hardly seen it but yes that's
what trust is.*

And this is what my country must be knows Letty Catts
the girl who writes the songs.

The decade ends.

In newsreels here's the truth: as file upon ecstatic file
of *volk* are rasped to arms, our stoush gets declared
in sad avuncular cadences.

Now, though, girls stand four-square,
hand-on-hip confident, Jean Arthur style.

'This *Never Never*,' one of them guesses, 'that Letty's writing:
it exists,' she understands, 'it'll be a true, great reason for fighting.'

A Brown Slouch Hat

for Cheryl Pisterman

We're to imagine this: a time when anyone from Queensland
         writing to Deanna Durbin
receives a reply straight from the set of 'Three Smart Girls';
or this (a few years later, still waiting for those truly worthwhile days,
not much occurring but in slow, warm, big town Brisbane
something's always growing): she's heard on the wireless: a probable
         floosie of your age,
but patriotic, and with more front than any window dresser ever requires
         is urging
'Rally around, Australia! Let's do our bit! We've a war to win!'
And yes yes yes you know what she means!
       So imagine all this as how it
         begins:
our story of Brenda and Dot: two smart Queensland girls
(schoolkids who loved the idea of dropping lines to the stars,
steno-secs who know their Daphne Du Maurier and Eleanor Dark,
women who'll give their children easy, adaptable names like Cheryl and
         Alan) who enlist,
then go into Cipher, turn out as NCOs (they'll always turn out as NCOs!)
who, meeting in wartime, start that adventure friendship always should be…

Girls on the Avenue

Waddayamean you've never seen *Pure Shit?*
A titles-to-credits rampage of black Melbourne wit

meets the scorers and the scored: so so so beyond bewdy
seeing it's near enough to a patriotic duty.

And here's where the girls come in: permed, waxed, douched and flossed,
once the avenue's crossed

they'll be slippin' up o-kay! (There's a fortune a day
just pulling cocks!) Whilst here, in that washed and grainy way

we are just are, the story so far: I'm alive you're alive,
and if this isn't '74 this sure is '75,

the dawning of The Age of Near Enough Victimless Sin
(which is, as I've said, where the girls come in).

Don't *But but but but* me sport. It's obscene
you've never caught *Pure Shit*…waddayamean?

My Old Man's a Groovy Old Man

...and the old girl's macro stroppy, razor honed.
So shouldn't I just go out, score heaps and get us both totally stoned?

Like, her ex my dad my dad, that alpha and omega pisser,
has run off to the Sunshine Coast with...Larissa?

Okay 'lurv'. I kinda admire it, but I'd rather go dead
than think my best friend could be giving my father...head?

So, when I get to see him and he's all earstud 'n' lovebite
(hoho, whose been helping *you* co-dependent through the night?)

and familial interaction seems the least of his chores:
'Err how's y'mother, Princess?' Jeez Pop, jeez Pop, how's yours?

The embarrassment! He's fifty one, she's twenty four,
so wouldn't you move further than Maroochydore?

There's better, it's worse but, the *Get this!* fun begins.
They run this motel, see? And she's expecting, she's expecting...twins?

Bound for Botany Bay

for Daniel Willis
after *Blue Murder*

Here fellow Aussies, good 'n' ready: the gospel that accords with
Neddy.
Payouts? Paybacks? Shots to dodge? Better you check first with Rog.
Cash gets raked-in by the acres, if you're matey with The Breakers.
Sure they'll barter, threaten, wheedle, but junkies crawl home to
the needle.
Sallie-Anne was quite a lay, she could sidle and sashay.
But when the end came for Lanfranchi, Huckstepp hollered like a banshee.
Media bound went silly Sallie, made her life a one-way alley.
Though they've solemn obligations hitmen too have limitations.
How many reasons eased out Flannery? (Count the grains to fill a granary!)
He's working out the mighty if, buried under Kingsford-Smith.
Cop 'n' crim packed as she ought, the First Fleet's sailing into port.
Dogs catch fleas, cats grow mange, so who says there's been *any* change?
Roger rules and Ned prevails: we invented New South Wales!
Anti-heroes loved by plebs are celeb-crims not crim-celebs.

A World of Our Own

Will Claire attend the Boat Race dance?
Have I a pre-selection chance?

In my study Nigel twitched:
'It's Lucy, Dad, we must get hitched.'

And I, to ease us from this jolt,
poured both a treble single malt.

Name the ratio, what's the blend
of house guests for a Lorne weekend?

But Fleur's a gem since up she musters
professors, senators, messrs justice.

Whilst life improves upon 'all right'
if I can make an Old Boys night.

Angus and Polly were around
that Sunday when the PM drowned.

I Go To Rio

If ya got it flaunt it
Liberace

Since everything old is always turning neo: g'day Peter (this is Alan,
chum,
songwriter manqué, author of these stanzas)...future Oz icon from Fitzroy
through to Freo,
with bodytalk more pirouette than scrum, and freckled with chutzpah, see
him, off he prances
(as if born under Samuel Goldwyn's Leo) straight to the daughter of Frank
and Ethel Gumm
(the world knows Judy, who remembers Frances?); then playing Antony to
her Liza's Cleo
(after you'd been half-courted by the mum) and, finding what a boy might
do, took chances
in all that Seventies turning Eighties brio, high kick both legs, twirl round
and shake y' bum
with lines of Radio City Rockette dancers; or entertaining on your *O sole mio*
in cabaret, bath house, that land of Kingdom Cum, which face it wasn't
Tenterfield or Kansas;
only to cop one slow ugly cheerio: like when, in a Carioca slum,
a hit squad advances, and they (as you) need miracles worthy of Padre Pio...
and still it snares with relentless taraa-tarum, and all that's feared is death
has the only answers.
Maybe. But, at the Maracanã, when *I* went to Rio, we saw that the players
could march to this: their banner's differing drum:
PARE DE POR FAVOR MATAR NOSSAS CRIANÇAS

Bad Habits

...I take the hap
Of all my deeds.
George Meredith, *Modern Love* XX

2.50 what? The night's at kickback stage.
And if I'm the man heading to LAX
you must be Madison, monument to your sex,
sweet, groomed, worldly and my daughter's age,
with cute, white slivers of *k'thwack k'thwack*
for hours of bug-eyed frenzy.
                                        Till the chop.
And 'Ken,' I'm hearing, 'reckon we oughta stop,
or name us a worse place for your heart attack.'
        But bad and badder habits hunt in packs:
if y'urge says *Go!* so y'splurge y'dough
oh ain't that par for one horny CEO
who craves you as his item-to-the-max
(unless, well hardly, you've turned out a narc).
        I queue at 6 with Trans-Pacific rabble.
Till then Mmmadison: you straddle I babble:
bloodshot, out-staring Fox Sports in the dark.

Love is in the Air

for Ava Drew, speaker of this poem 2040

       Pausing the footage with bemusing patience
See that couple dancing? They're my folks!
with thirty-to-sixty-year-old hits and jokes
marking the fold-unfold-and-fold of generations,
it's mine to announce, as I view this wedding
-who may as well be (if not exactly) there-
that day love was, you guessed it, in the air:
'Ha ha kids, *I* know where you're heading:
change with all of its romance and power...
yes call it love, *moi* as result (ahem...)'
who, knowing there's places in body, soul and brain
untainted by the fractious or the sour,
will once more cry *That's them, that's truly them!*
Filled with our future, Red Bull and Champagne!

My Home Among the Gum Trees

for Phillip Hall
from *Blackburn, the Movie*

Because I find the condescension of posterity — through which we applaud
ourselves by imposing our enlightened standards on a supposedly benighted
past — to be a particularly unattractive reflex…

Benjamin Schwarz

Outside the station two Peace Crusaders, lean and scrawny as Sidney and
Beatrice Webb, distribute handbills;

the Group Captain, equally lean but snipped to an official trim, nods
slightly, declining the pamphlets;

as his acquaintance, the tubby City Councillor informs what's already
known about the pair:

'Just checking of course, but no-one who truly matters has actually *seen*
their house, bush everywhere…

Still, the man has ideas on what's unique: 'Ten tiny miles from town, yet
trees do give this place its stamp…'

Then as the Vicar putts by on his motorcycle the Group Captain gives a
much more measured nod, mouthing *Padre*;

whilst here's that pest, that self-appointed Worker who gets any decent
chap to ask: 'What's this joker doing here, wasn't his train supposed to be an
hour ago?'

And like any joker the Worker has his question too: 'So you *saw service*,
well who didn't? And what remains of yours, Group Captain? Some stupid
un-Australian mustache!'

'…its stamp, our signature,' the Councillor continues, 'we just don't seem
that ready to dismantle the bush, perhaps we never will…'

And having his fill the Group Captain closes with 'Doubtless.'

And doubtless too, as on any weekday morning, from Main Street,
South Parade and the subway felt-hatted young men are hanging
their bikes whilst stenographers in summer frocks descend from the
bus;

though back in the kitchens, radios today might well suspend
or at least limit Leroy Anderson's jaunty 'Jazz Legato', the Ames
Brothers' dippy if infectious 'Ragg Mopp'.

For later on the bus, seeing a copy of *The Age* or *The Argus*
bordered in black, I'll be asking my mother 'Why?'

Friday February 8 1952. 'The King has died.'

Metropolitan Poems
and Other Poems

Chatswood: Ruth Nash Speaks.

Among those attending Ken and Ruth Nash's New Year's Eve Party were Ken's work colleagues Gib Bogle and Geoffrey Chandler, and Chandler's wife Margaret. On the morning of January 1, 1963, Gib and Margaret were found dead, poisoned, beside the Lane Cove River. Poison and poisoner were never identified.

...and we are, in best sellers or movies, near press-ganged to pretend
how simple, bland beginnings might prologue a ludicrous end,

so there's Gib on arrival lightfooting it down our hall,
and there's Gib a day later lightfooting bugger all.

We think we know the limits? We're merely to follow this text:
Lives unfold lives fold, here's one hour here's the next.

And where in a plot place 'the heavens', their ever-expanding No?
Well you barely ask such questions of the CSIRO,

for (lab coats, leather patches, pipes and British cars)
my other half worked with boffins who rarely trusted the stars.

Though let's say alignments were ordered, and on his last night alive,
always that hub of attention Gib is first to arrive.

Might the knocker he raps signal start not end? Alarm? What alarm?
Take no offence give no offence, that is Gib and his charm.

Look at the time before Christmas when innocence was rife,
and bemused by possibilities he first met Chandler's wife:

we were there for that fol-de-rol, we saw how he'd basked
in this shy young housewife's sweet warm blaze. 'Invite 'em both?' Gib asked.

So half an hour on came the couple: her small-frame floral skirt;
his beard we might accommodate- but sandals? Hawaiian shirt?

'Jacket and tie were requested...' my spouse was tingeing red.
As his mutters entered their threshold 'Oh lighten up Ken,' I said.

(But wanting my man a serious man, if times like this it showed,
let him mix and pour the drinks, make mine the etiquette load.)

Then, offering merest shadows to what *he* might be about,
dismissing himself from 12 Waratah Street, Chandler strolled out.

Where'd *we* place such affection, what side of ridgey-didge?
Off to buy cigarettes some place…over the Harbour Bridge?

But with our 'at home' assembling and a new year arriving,
us Nashes gave little regard to Chandler out there, driving…

on our night to not-quite-remember when, gentility set to prevail
we headed three, four, five, six, up quite a low-key scale:

Ken running the bar till midnight, not even a conga line,
we crossed arms as our parents might for the days of auld lang syne.

With the hour for tradition over, shelving the coy and discreet
I urged Gib to the dance floor (our party to its feet).

How could you (this much into a year) ever package and carry regrets?
So we stamped out a quasi flamenco as I jiggled castanets.

And who is that proving he'd like to…but can't quite…why it's…
Dr Bogle, as hipster, cutting a rug with The Twist!

Then, our evening remodulating back to its chatty tone,
there he is seeking out Margaret. Well both it seems were alone.

With his wife at home nursing might he be given the chance
to indulge in a harmless night of lightweight suburban romance?

Wide-eyed for what's still possible, getting a grip on each fad,
so he was playing the lad? Well Gib was always the lad!

And where was *her* need to simper, serenely self efface?
It was New Year's Eve in Chatswood, Chatswood's a grown up place.

Till cashing in those dividends absence feels it has earned,
after his half the night elsewhere Chandler returned.

And here at my home a transaction (making what passes for sense
to the North Shore/ Sydney/ Australia's genteel prurience):

two men were discussing softly the where, the when and the who
and if you'd give more than a passing shrug well I say woopy-doo:

we'd soon know again those limits to whatever wasn't and was;
how in all explanations you would finish each sentence 'Because...'

Gib would drive home Margaret; and having her bestowed,
our party was over for Chandler, he went back to the road.

And glancing away such arrangements that, I gathered, was that.
(Who *were* you Mrs Chandler? we never got round to a chat.)

For this might be the second (the last) time Gib and Margaret met,
but wouldn't you think by 4AM the details were ours to forget?

Instead they kept piling higher to their inconclusive amen
(such as we'd be informing Mr Loomes SM)

when only trusting to trivia, trivia stayed in the dock:
a grubby, green Ford Prefect sedan? an SSW frock?

And it still feels odd to consider some malevolent star had planned,
for early 1963, this most famous event in the land,

informing that crew of gate-crashers Messrs Malice/ Accident/ Fate:
'The fun starts around a quarter to nine, oh and ladies, please bring a plate.'

And we might shut the door on reporters, might firmly lower the sash,
but the whole town now had opinions on those seven hours Chez Nash.

In that best time for dying, hour for being born,
with the milkman and the milkman's horse treading out of the dawn,

whilst Ken and I stay busy farewelling our twenty guests
(this hour gives no time to anticipate fortune's idiot jests)

Gib and the Ford are waiting, Margaret walks to our gate
(who'll ever understand there is no early now or late?)

she's only to follow instructions a final star might give:
just turn left into Waratah Street, and a few more hours to live.

The God of Nope

for David Greason (1961-2011)

Founded by Australian tax lawyer Frank Nugan and former Green Beret Michael Hand, the Nugan Hand Bank was a leading money launderer of the 1970s with very strong links to and between the CIA and drug based transnational organized crime. Nugan suicided, Hand fled to the US and a onetime junior partner recalls.

1

One part vocation matching nine parts lurk,
where was a future stuck in pipsqueak work?
Young man in my mirror weren't that kind of jerk.

Possessing horse sense how y'damn thing plays,
to itemise and seize each current craze,
young man churned through his most ambitious phase.

Sure, we were younger then, but understand
we're always younger 'then', 'then' is its brand.
And 'then' was a mighty 'now!' for Nugan Hand.

2

'If sought,' says Mike, 'I'm well known enough,
master of both called and not called bluff.
Frank though is natural for our front man stuff.

Two Dukes of Nouse we recognized your gift
to catch an opening, scamper through the rift.
Our noun is product and our verb is shift.

For war's no fuckfest pilfered from robotics:
heart, gut or prick, obey your own erotics.
You'll hear,' shrugs he, 'rumours of narcotics...

Some place, we're told, there has to be a law
which may apply to us and may not, for
this now's our world at play/ at prayer/ at war.

Eyeballing Tyranny? Rinsing out the dope?
Why be a martyr to the God of Nope
when yeah! blooms forth from every boomboom! hope?

We just suggest, the world falls in line…'

3

      And *Hard to know what is or is not mine*
that's how my life got lived till '79.

What dawn was yours? Why every single dawn
raised our marquees to occupy each lawn.
Ahh to be present as a bank gets born:

by Griffith shysters out of Bircher cranks,
go-getter got 'ems out of the middle ranks.
In a world fast-filling with y' Mikes 'n' Franks,

y' Bernies 'n' Buddys through to Aussie Bob,
(the prince, the ponce, the sybarite and slob)
weren't we just one most eclectic mob

toasting our brand of Liberty; and yup,
no way that's us who'd been flogged a pup,
but deadshits in some lounge-room shooting up.

Who'd guess first off meeting Frank 'n' Mike
them as part of Democracy's epic hike
from Chang Mai to Luanda via the spike?

Call me naïve though never term me stooge.
Lapels or dividends? Both exceeded huge.
Who knows what size *après* that *deluge*

when Nugan hit his dashboard with a clunk,
when *Oo-roo Aussie* Hand just did his bunk,
when Freedom conquered, courtesy of junk?

4

      This be our law: to blast what we erect.
(Call it existence? What else you expect?).
Dialled for an escort, trusting we'd connect.

And after being both john-'n'-working-girled,
my occupation's innocently unfurled:
'I work for conmen wired to save the world.

It's *Guns for Je-sus!* time! Each day I jive
with two of the top gun Je-sus men alive:
bankers with haircuts pinched from the Dave Clark Five.'

      More girl next door than par for a Sydney hooker,
freckled yet groomed, you know the kind of looker.
The outfit held this seminar, I took her.

But fall-guy for every passing lacy panty
(and this on that evening Frank went extra-ranty)
quite possibly I'd over-upped my ante.

      'You know,' smirks she, 'the loony bin's in session,
when sleaze meets God meets guns meets manic depression.
Makes a chick proud hers is the true profession.'

      For here was Frank: hero, brother, boss,
his rolled gold ideals sluicing off as dross,
haranguing like he's up there, on the cross:

'All moral centres have turned multi-polar,
'cause strike after strike like an A-plus ten-pin bowler
the Reds obliterate Afghanistan, Angola!

From Patagonia to the Golan Heights
our false twin with all its satellites
chomps up the Free World with enlarging bites!

Behold a vulture gulping down…a dove!'
(Such push was bad enough, here came the shove.)
'Whilst ours is a world we're freeing…out of love!'

Then as bikies commandeer the road,
or like some stud set to shoot his load,
re-enter Mike in *Hiya Fella!* mode:

'Oh slay me Frank your mammoth hahaha
takes up the tab for our entire bar!
After which we'll resurrect the Tsar!

Hot damn, fuck yeah, bloody oath 'n' zwounds!
Open ye portals and let loose all hounds!'
  I had a hunch these were final rounds,

learning at last all rounds return as rout
-behold this mortal deal, that poisoned shout-
for thus came the shout: 'Get out get out get out!'

5

  With zeal dispersing every useless creed
(who has the gall to itemise it 'greed'?)
we'd worshipped though the God of Nope indeed:

better than pokies Mike shovelling off the lot,
Frank's puzzled dictum 'Plot? We have some plot?'
Benchmarks for huh? Best never ask *Just what?*

Nope was our license, our intoxication,
all white heat vigilance *sans* obligation,
freeing a world through extermination,

making that constant love of quarry, quest,
an I-mean-everyday blast-to-your-chest,
after which, wouldn't you need a rest?

One thought it best his brains got cleansed with lead.
The other's progress hovers round 'Less said…'
(he likes it that way).
    Meanwhile see me wed

(with innocent panache of a cleared defendant

and near obligatory shark's tooth pendant)
a frisky, leggy, doe-eyed flight attendant

who (know what it's like getting your psyche scrubbed,
health-farm-rehab rubba-dub-dub-dubbed?)
oversaw a re-emerging me, hot-tubbed

and Perrier-pure, blessed past the power of ten,
with mellowed verve courtesy of Zen
informing all it's time to start again.

As few choose their heavens (if most their respective hells)
-locate some 'centre', soon an aura jells-
better than 'someone' you'll turn 'someone else'.

Enter 'closure', exit merchant banking,
I grant to Karma every hour a thanking
and give myself this adjectival ranking:

ecstatic-bland. Nothing's remotely 'rife'
where *we* exist (love you to meet the wife).
Your work? Your name? Wouldn't you change your *life*?

        Fortune or fate or focus: see how my luck is
holding still? Why not, when all the ruckus
lies thirty years behind but (so long) suckers,

it stands to an unending fine-tuned reason
that ours were modes appropriate to season.
        How could...no I *dare* you call it treason!

        (Whatever past you had, wipe out that section.
You were no witness, you need what protection?
Fiction must have spun you such confection.)

Neutral Bay

The speaker was a courier for the Mr Asia Drug Syndicate

I'd get in from the airport after midnight
and wait a day, till someone came around,
unloaded me and made me *Thanks sweetheart*
$15,000 richer. Then I'd hardly be noticed,
not till Allison called, or Kay, and we went off to buy
all these incredible clothes.
        I knew of two apartments, ours and theirs;
theirs, a place where you went in,
(saw The Organization dropping by to pack the stuff)
and you went out.
                What did I think I was,
not old enough to break the law? What law?
By then the only law I had to keep
was getting away with knowing Terry Clark,
so yes I was old enough. I did it,
did it often enough; and whoever I was
I just needed an identity, even if
I didn't need an identity. I was smart and
waiting about on the fringes of Terry Clark's
banal life, hardly knew what I did,
except that I was that damn special.
        Giving myself a week away from spending
I caught a light aircraft back to the folks,
stayed up to near midnight
doing gossip with Mum. Of course
someone's kid was 'into drugs',
always someone's kid and always drugs.
        And I thought
Who knows what The Organization's doing
right now: cutting, grinding and packing;
delivering, collecting and waiting
and how I never wanted to feel damn special again.
But *Thanks a lot sweetheart* of course I did.

A Portrait of Three Young High School Teachers

In full, pleated, white or floral-patterned skirts,
you're twenty-six, twenty-four or twenty:
the focused one, the one who's sharp-tongue wise
and the newly-wed from interstate
whom the other two can't help but protect and advise.

And if like the nation this school seems
on better days almost miraculously do-it-yourself,
doubtless that's because who else is there to do it?
(Then, if you wish to appear old fashioned
it's all like a 'courtship', or what you're discovering re marriage.)

Whilst 'This,' waves forth your supercilious headmaster,
'all this is how we like our things round here...'
He reminds some of Raymond Huntley, pauses and nods
as he calls you by the collective 'Mesdames'
and laughs, never at himself, only his quips.

'Indeed,' comes Ruth's later response, 'how we like our things...'
'I'm sure we'll work around it,' says Yvonne
with her innate knowledge of working around.
Which they will, though by winter Frances craves
a few adjustments: 'If only they'd let us wear slacks!

Can you imagine wearing anything else?'
But on this afternoon, in a new year
at a new school, whose tiresome Latin motto
you'd like to think might be interpreted as
Making Do With What We've Got (which isn't much)

some things you're hoping to commence will commence.
And if outside, starting at Holland Road
(after which they'll circle out into those whatever-beyonds)
the instant museum of jingles and choruses, slogans and chants
continue their parade:

a Peace Congress for both civic-minded and pest,
or for the troubled, the naïve, the plain inquisitive,
Revival Crusades making sure of merely nothing-
friendships can at least delay these dour, sour uncertainties
of annihilation and damnation, can't they?

They better. So, walking to their staffroom
Ruth, a young woman at her most formally informal
tells Frances: 'A few folk are coming over
this Saturday. Yvonne and her fiancé will be there.
You and your husband are very, very welcome.'

A High School Staff Room, Melbourne's Northern Suburbs, Winter 1977

'Yes girls, can we help?' All *umm 'n' err*,
propped in our doorway: Linda and Simone
(one with the tighter, one the shorter dress)
peering at grown-ups. Kids don't waste the guess,
rejoice it still remains a less-than-known:
that musty, meagre world of Miss and Sir.
Ours is a life where offered half a chance
him, her or him are yanking off your pants.

No? Well pardon my gall-coated laughter
but second term hasn't 'only just begun':
it's slow and sodden late July. And please
I want to talk about the Vietnamese,
who did just two things: kicked us out and won.
Though, patterns never lying, not long after
the vanity, the malice and the folly
disposed of Jim Cairns' stoic melancholy.

Each day less raw but each day extra honed
the girls piss off. Tomorrow is beginning.
'The Northern Suburbs yep true coalface stuff,
puberty plus and wow that Linda's rough.
What school is this?' Fumey, pin-eyed, grinning,
today's E.T. (I'll stand any bet) is stoned.
'The station's what way…right? We'll make it fine
but…is this the Epping or the Upfield line?'

Breakfast with Darky

A middle-aged high school teacher, Melbourne, the late 1970s

Often parking when I visit Kim
I recall this other car:
the one that returned to prop outside
our place, Marj and mine, in Ascot Vale.
        'Don't tell me,' I forgive myself,
'I'm starting to feel just like those spooks
of twenty years ago...the ones
(not dimwitted, not even thuggish)
I tried to write about in
'Just Doing My Job'
the flagship story of my first, my finest,
make that my one collection.

                    *

At the appropriate committee
the chairman felt I'd been too kind.
        'Without the working class,' he fantasized,
'that lot would slit our throats.
Of course you have to wonder what's
inside a rapist's mind, a priest's, a spook's...
you do it well though...' and,
as his mind changed gears, 'Well I suppose
they're victims too...' (well they weren't) and,
before he could be halted,
headed into closing mode:
'Now what was it that Lenin said...?'

                    *

I've never been a spook of course
and these days, catching me parking
outside Kim's, am just a father
visiting his daughter.

                    *

Early one school year Mike,
a young newcomer, sought me out:
saying my name then saying my name again:
'Does anyone round here know who you are,
who you really are?'
                              Macho, bustling with it,
he had a loud, a very loud
matey integrity. His job, I was advised,
was making sure the kids he taught
both read and wrote. I liked him
and he (he used the word) 'Adored'
Just Doing My Job: Stories from the Struggle.
Hadn't the Special Branch
'Those pale, pinched men in gabardine...'
been buried by my sheer humanity?
                    Mike was so sincere, so fragile with it,
I couldn't bother to advise:
'In the end I only wrote what the party
wanted. Quitting that much of my life
required...how much heroics?
Just one. One on a day I would not
be labeled. Simple? Yes simple.'
                    Though I might've told him next time:
'Bugger the form guide. Every smoko
didn't Darky Nolan reach for the very latest
in realist writing, just as they were doing
in Bulgaria?'
                    But Mike never fawned.
And he if anyone might still enjoy
Breakfast with Darky and other stories
typed neat in their manila folder,
waiting in a drawer, our very special
What's the use tell me what's the flamin' use?
Australian samizdat.

                    *

Outside Darky's
like outside ours, there often parked
a spook. So one morning, feeling for the man,
he trolleys out fruit, cereal, toast and tea
with 'How'd we like our eggs today,
eh comrade?' Poor spook, poor so poker-
faced, with all that golden rule rammed
right up him, spook.
                    The struggle too had spooks.
          'Yes yes,' the committee would concede
(and Marj served on this committee)
'yes yes a fine adventurist game,
yes yes might make a brilliant skit on
Sunnyside Up...' But no no,
didn't Comrade Nolan truly understand
we're at war and our warning is
Don't serve spooks, serve the only class
that matters!
                    Would we'd all been warned
just how much game (and not just Darky's)
life had become: their spooks, our spooks,
and every committee: all game.
          Which is what my story said.

                              *

          Marj shook her head:
'I always knew you were...' and giving out
her weak, wan smile, 'a capitalist roader!'
          If it arrives from no matter where
(managing directors, elected representatives,
the foreman, your spouse, history itself)
there are some, the truly lucky few who,
first time they hear it, already know
Friends, we're listening to a cliché!
And for more than any 'class that matters'
I wrote for that small few.

                              *

                    In Ascot Vale,
on kero-heater nights, just made
for the very coldest war, I'd worked
at what's required to be
a wiz-kid, vanguard realist writer.
Succeeded. Stopped.
                    So that later,
years later, Mike could tell me: 'Those days
bred near-giants: Hardy mate, Waten, Morrison
sure…but you, you were writing
the history of our future. What happened, mate?'
            And if I wished I could've asked
'You are meaning what?'
but liking the man only had the wistful
energy to answer: 'Mike, the future had arrived.
'Breakfast with Darky': who'd publish that?
Quadrant? For the wrong reasons,
and even if they were the right ones
I still believe in self respect…'

                    *

            I had to.
Imagine having a wife, a comrade,
who not just left you but
went to try and redeem Darky Nolan,
wean him off the neddies,
turn him from proletarian court jester
to indispensable leadership-group cog.
            What is a game if not that?
            Well this: a half life as elected rep,
from one staffroom to the next,
accommodating all who would've once passed
as 'enemy': the insisting principal who has
'Not haha immodest claims…';
his deputy whose only interactions
all seem to end in 'No seriously folks…';
some lady coordinator whose faith proclaims
'There's lots to admire in today's Top Forty…'

*

Or this game: with some try hard
jazz band merging in their fashion
The Internationale with *Didn't He Ramble*,
and a waterfront heavyweight
part bellowing/part blubbering 'On yer Darkeee!'
and me biting my tongue knowing
that goose down there in his purple suit
with overdone lapels, that mega-goose
was chosen (no other word)
to be the second (more appropriate)
Mr. Marj.
      (Ahh Marj, ever loving, evermore
correct line, fully indignant, spook-hating Marj:
when we turn into a People's Australia
you'll head the secret police!)
      With the deceased
hardly the type for eulogies the afternoon
would give us tales, Darky tales:
heckling in 'a robust if predictable
Marxist vernacular';
on the Bulgarian Friendship delegation
and getting lost (thirty six hours mind!)
in Plovdiv; Darky hardly coping but
really trying with Women's Lib;
Darky as stepdad well yes as stepdad;
Darky, the spook and that legendary breakfast.
      And walking from the wake Kim got told:
'Well Darky always meant it!'
             Not so.
'He was a fuckwit, Dad. You ever seen him
in that suit at some trash 'n' treasure?
And going on how everyone was proud I went
To Uni High. And pleading things like
Show your father gratitude.
What do the bosses do with all *their* Darkys, Dad?'

*

From the community centre
the songs that Darky sang spread
into the late spring evening.
(If you didn't know them word-
by-word you might've sworn them
to be vaudeville.)
          'What do the bosses do
with all *their* Darkys? Parliament, Kim.'

They Came to Moorabbin

Just after she turned twenty,
when the War was nearly three years old,
Iris joined the AWAS: an adventurous choice
and a sensible one for her, Dot, Elwyn, Gwen,
that generation of unadorned-names girls,
Jean and Elaine, Nance and Wynne.

                          Later,
at some regimental hop, Iris met Keith,
who fibbed about his age, first to the army
then to her, but who seemed to say
what she considered correct things:
the outline of his plans, for one.

        And being adaptable Iris could adjust
(that's what she knew Keith liked in her)
as his plans became their Post War plans,
and the Post War plans turned opinions, his opinions,
then reactions, then demands, particularly demands.
And this was when all visits to his brother
(and very soon his mother) ceased.

                     That same winter,
one mild Sunday afternoon with their three boys
at Half Moon Bay, Iris recognized her:
Nance, Nance Bliss, someone she had slightly known
in Cipher, a mother of four who soon informed
'He died last year, my husband.
You may have known him Iris, from the War,
Tony Conway, who became a diplomat…'

*

That day this trio settled it:
Nance with her minimal desire for charity
but always accepting friendship,
Iris appreciating someone new and interesting,
and Keith (hoping to maintain his need
for being needed) who could be useful:
fixing her taxes for one thing,
whilst the children, hers and theirs,

bound by little more than some trip to the beach,
were courtesy cousins now, friendly
if hardly 'made for each other' friends.

      So soon, another Sunday afternoon,
see in that twelve mile trip to Moorabbin
Iris and Keith sensing Nance to be
just that touch removed from their more
'comfortable' friends: the Vineys, the Izzards,
the Dobsons, the Prices.

                   'I've got over some of it...'
and she was shrugging. 'The children help of course,
but...but...' And the shrugs continued,
leaving her new friends to understand
What else in this woman's life has ever been
so unique? Nothing at all.

      Following his funeral Nance knew
she must be playing any amount of roles
(what adjustments wouldn't be required
as a diplomat's wife turned Moorabbin widow?)
for if hers was a roomy, weatherboard villa,
'I'm no Martian,' she'd inform, 'but here I live on Mars.'

      Tony's death must belong to Nance,
who else need wallow in it?
Once you felt sorry for any others feeling sorry
for you, where then would such sorrows cease?
Which was why she took to them:
Iris and Keith knew her, Nance, not Nance and Tony,
and a new small part of her life could now commence.
It had to, even if Keith would greet
'Hi Toots!' and farewell 'Bye Toots!' so half of Mars
would hear him.

              If she's my age knew Iris
that much more has happened to her:
wartime and beyond when so many women saw
death demanding of their men:
'Now you're marching off with us.'
Which hadn't yet been Keith.

           Nance she recalled,
came from a different crowd to hers
(and Dot, Elwyn, Gwen and Wynne's).

Here was a woman good (or much too good?)
with men, so that when Corporal Bliss meets
Major Conway, fifteen years older, divorced,
and set to recommence in External Affairs,
would she like to join him? Yes she would in
Wellington, Edinburgh, Cape Town and Moorabbin,
where he dies.
        And where he remains,
trim and balding, shaking hands with Mr Menzies,
framed and mounted on the mantelpiece
(always gets the visitors bemused does Mr Menzies).
        First though Nance in her Nance way
will tell her friends: 'My father was a teacher,
his running gag was school inspectors...' and
'If I'm not middle-aged today I'll sure be middle-
aged tomorrow...' and 'Now call me a sophisticate,
but what sophisticate's a Moorabbin sophisticate?'
And then 'If at night,' she won't mind confessing,
'my eldest two should find me teary,
here's hoping they will understand,
although I'm sure the only time death gets understood
is when you've reached there.' She'll pause and ask herself,
'A bitch? I'm not that touch more bitchier than many but
I have to be, I must, my children need their lives now.'
        Later she'd be telling Iris (and only her)
'...his first marriage flopped i.e. little happened.
The War helped close it. When I met him Tony craved
for change, so I gave into the exotic life
of a diplomat's wife. Cape Town and our consulate?
Think proteas and marble floors with staff provided.
And yes there were slivers of glamour,' Nance confided.
'Black nannies to prop the slim young wife-with-martini,
the not so slim young mum with three-make-it-four
in seven years.'
        Then after Tony got invalided home
they came to Moorabbin where, as a diplomat's widow
you really are exotica and (what a choice!)
either a snob or not.
        That's where Iris mattered:
you could let loose your hidden snob with her,

who was loyal and never deserved to be a target.
Some weekdays Nance packed up her youngest two
and drove to this good sport, top scout, great chum
who had the measure of the Women's Pages,
who liked checking the star signs for fun
(though five minutes on forgetting what was written)
who understood all that slapstick potential
chatting with Nance entailed,
who, unlike the Martians knew it was
So nice to have a man around the house...

    When as a friend, a visitor or host, Nance hearing Keith
believed him to be the kind of man that she might deal with;
the times were still Post War enough and little seemed
more Post War and less like Mars than Keith:
wanting something to believe in, and how he could transform
beliefs into opinions: the individual and family, his family,
your family and *Know* he'd always emphasise
what you're talking about be it free enterprise growth for
an unlimited Australia, the British Commonwealth of Nations,
or even the Match of the Day, that's right,
Know what you're talking about or failing that
make it perfectly understood one has one's beliefs
(though if one found one had overreached
one might fall back upon *Oh no no no I never said
exactly that!*).

    Though *Iris*, a girl friend wouldn't even
barely ask *why did you marry him?*

        And, as if in reply
to such an absent question, this would have arrived
*Because that's my enigma, and you nor anyone
will never solve it.*

    'My children,' Nance was asking,
'maybe there's not too much to worry over?
Though imagine if there is I'm hardly certain what.'

    'If,' Iris answered, 'your father dies
when you are six (mine did, pneumonia)
you just step around it for you need to...'

    Well she's a stoic Nance thought,
*though if I sat as she does (ever pleasant ever pleasing)
to marinate in Keith's opinionating,*

wouldn't my time be ulcer time!
                         True, yet something
in the widow thrived with him. That something
also saying *Please never lay a hand on me,*
I'd lose Iris, I'd lose Tony, and if I've had it with
that stuff and you know what is meant by 'that stuff',
in all the variety of mourning this'll be my mourning,
Moorabbin style.
        Then Keith started visiting, weekdays
(the taxes and what else) telling Toots
she looked like Lauren Bacall, which was nice.
        'I'm no June Allyson,' she mock-confessed,
nor Mitzi Gaynor even less.' True Kay Kendall
might've been auditioned, but with her strong, worldly-
wise eyes Betty Bacall sounded fine. 'And why not,' she riffed,
'Celeste Holm or Glynis Johns for Iris?
And if you want a star for Tony, think Trevor Howard:
all that officer's necessity to play it correct
with just a hell-raiser's touch, then possibly not,
probably not, till one day just as surely never.
I loved him, nursed and loved him...' and she
would never love-and-nurse another,
since Nance loathed dying, Tony's dying and sometimes
even him for dying.
                And how might Miss Holm or Miss Johns
take to their husbands visiting a certain Miss Bacall?
Sports, scouts and chums (always trusting,
forever understanding) needed to be protected,
Nance knew that much and knew her limits.
Though she could imagine Keith informing Iris how
that afternoon he'd just dropped by Moorabbin
(nothing else for there was nothing else)
and in the telling, enjoying it, allowing his wife
to plain soak up any ambiguity she thought was there,
any envy she might be making out of it.
After which who knew what tensions might result,
what balances have to get regained?
        Yet they continued to connect, Keith and Nance,
almost as if they had to, though by now her tragedies,
portrayed as oh-so-matter-of-fact,

helped him in overreacting to his own. Item:
such things as what his brother did:
doing Keith or the mother or both out of some late
great aunt's South Gippsland investment property,
when that place that place should've been heading
his way, since doesn't it come down to this:
it's the individual that always matters,
and given Keith's an individual, lest we forget
all those Little Sir Echoes rising through the ranks
of his party, the *Party of the Individual* and,
Nance must be told, he's sure not one of them
and no (he motions to the mantelpiece)
he and Mr Menzies haven't met, one day though
they might.
        How do widows adjust?
Now that interests Iris, adding she trusts to her understanding,
enough that she's mentioning to Keith how the daughter
still sleeps with the mother. He though believes his wife
is making such an amount of what exactly?
She must return to his motto:
Know what you're talking about. Such as this:
when it comes to them, them as a family unit,
he knows she loves him, he has his career,
and with that career, life (their life) has been laid on,
that's fair isn't it?
        There was so much
Iris needn't do!
        'She,' Keith might be expounding,
'she doesn't have to do *that*, this one's a daughter of
our mod-con era, doesn't want to, either...'
Because, if you think it over, life today is scarcely what
our mothers went through: Australia is the individual,
the individual is Australia, and hadn't we seen the War
so folks need never think of anything else?
        'Possibly,' Nance muttered back to Keith,
Keith speaking for his Iris.
        Possibly?
He lets her say it since, except when Iris contradicts,
Keith rather likes an opinionated woman,
each brings out a similar boorish edginess

in the other.
              So here comes Nance
(are you ready Keith?) on how this town, their town
their *Goodbye Melbourne Town, Melbourne Town Goodbye*
has or hasn't come of age.
                       '*Sure in 1926*
the world gets told, if it can be bothered listening,
weren't we some backwater's backwater.
Now though… Now though?
Name another thirty years before, name thirty years ahead
and won't we still be saying
Oh my, haven't we caught up!
It's ludicrous all this HSV-7, this XVI Olympiad
bringing the world (the world!) to Melbourne,
let alone Moorabbin: '96, '26, '56, '86 and help us
if we've survived '16. The world?
Tony showed me the world for he was the world.
But now I've seen it like I've seen enough
Moorabbin Martians peeping over and squinting through
my fences. No Keith, I don't require that kind of world:
the one minding everybody's business but its own,
the one that calls how I spend my days *chain-smoking*,
which since Tony left cannot be helped.
 And if it's believed I soak my nights in Yalumba,
Aspros and Yalumba, I'll always attend to my kids first,
that's what widows must be for; and if Nance enjoys a man
for conversation, which she does, she does not need you
or any other putting his hand inside her blouse,
now if ever.
              And it's not for mere appearances
I am voting *Government*, but ever since nice Mr Menzies
arrived in Cape Town, to puff and speechify about
the consulate, like some school inspector,
I've thought he couldn't run the Village Glee Club.
Okay Keith, you would take him seriously,
but weren't you made for Mr Menzies, President Eisenhower,
the very Duke of Edinburgh: that entire school inspector
common touch? I might vote the way I do although a vote's
the only thing they're getting. Otherwise I'm Bolshie,
platinum Bolshie!' What has he heard? What has Keith heard?

and pausing Nance attempts to rectify with this:
'You too must appreciate it: needing squabbles,
like I need my sherry, my eldest needs his homework.'

Homework? She shouldn't have said that,
it only gets her knowing and re-knowing that if for some
Post War seems as the very best in years, they're equally the worst
for men like Keith who need but catch
(or think they have as no-one else has)
a clear, plain, terrifying word, derailing him alone.

So what's he heard?
That Nance believes his sons of eight of six of four
never do their homework! Never? He saw to it,
he saw to it!

Now this demands perspective,
so let's make this very much one of time and place.
Some of you must recall how every year,
on an early April Saturday, outside any newsagent,
the Sun News-Pictorial announces to Moorabbin,
Moorabbin and all the world IT'S ON AGAIN.
You know that one? Well meet today's equally as special
It's on again, and as Nance knows she doesn't need
one single *It* being *on* let alone *again*
from such as Keith. Hasn't she heard, seen and walked away
from this before: men who are so sure they're
being baited, bailed-up and baited,
till 'Keith' it must be asked, 'what are you hearing?
You overreact to just about the lot...'
(who'll turn away making sure they're hearing nothing).

And Tony was hardly that.
Nance knew him as an urbane, disciplined man,
who when he discovered he was dying
(with a fourth child still to be born)
set out to find and buy a home his family might
survive him in.

But then he was an officer and diplomat.
Iris too remembers Tony (if hardly knew him)
though she can't tell Keith who won't believe her.

'That Nance,' he tells his wife and sons,
'sometimes I know she's out to trap me...'
though thriving on their squabbles seems but a way of

letting her know *Watch me get out of this one, Nance!*
True he'll be the paragon family friend: visiting the widow,
taking her eldest to the footy, attending to her taxes,
which being more than mere correct is the only thing
It's decency! to do. Besides, he'll never have to live
with her.

        Might these have been our weak-willed years?
Perhaps, though post any war won't plenty surely wish
to opt for a complacent life? And might these easily
have been our strong-willed years, propped for many
by that vigilance we fought for?

        And there between both weak and strong wills
Iris makes her stand: 'Shall we return to Half Moon Bay?'

        'Let's not,' she's told.

                The wife suggests
a bigger house, to which her husband gets annoyed:
'All right all right we'll get one, one day...'

        And with his eldest soon for the Boy Scouts,
Nance's soon for Highett High School,
since he's back on Mars again, let's make Martian fun,
spruiking like some HSV-7 barker:
'Mr Taxman says *Anytime is Tax Time!*

                    And no need gloating
but how more democratic can a nation get
than when Mr Menzies and his *Party of the Individual*
wins yet again?

        Though beyond all this, Toots,
no-one must find fault with Iris, his Iris
(did she understand?) although Toots guesses that
each day to her face he's finding fault and faults
and she's guessing right.

        On their next visit Iris takes another stand,
her own small, tentative view
on what a woman such as Nance might do.

        'Oh...' sighs Keith and 'Oh...' her husband whines,
'as if you'd bloody know!'

                Never was Iris
more her friend than then, with Nance appreciating
she couldn't do a thing, realising that
I may know how to read you but from now on Keith,

I'll never know how to play you: a man oh so needing to be required
(made as much for widows as for wives).

Who some days later is out there in her kitchen,
yet again announcing: 'Taxes, Toots, taxes coming up!'

And as her mouth starts and continues drying
Nance rehearses *For all your repertoire of Toots,*
of Betty Bacall, your wife is my friend
and you will never speak to her like that
in front of me again. Which rehearsal never will be
acted out, for if there is a Keith she can't predict,
much worse there's one she can:
that tension in those men wishing they had been
the officers, who know they'll never be the diplomats
shaking Mr Menzies' hand.

If a canny friend had heard and seen
what Iris copped, she may have given her that slightest glance
which read *Can't help himself? Oh yes he can!*

Though it's that even cannier Nance who asks herself
If I follow through and take him truly take him on,
where would such a declamation pay out?
She's answering *On his wife.*

*

There'll still be tolerance,
a ten year tolerance bringing Iris, Keith and the boys
to Moorabbin, but it's a fading tolerance,
and Nance will quit understanding *that Keith*, except
as someone oh so able to produce his portion of
their mutual grit; and for a bonus getting herself to believe
Wasn't it enough he kept his hands away from me
and did my taxes? Somebody had to.
                                          Till one day
that Keith having his fill of *that Nance*
(someone Iris recalled from AWAS,
someone she met at the beach) leaves and won't return.

All that remains are cards,
the annual women's ritual of greeting cards,
which finishes when Iris dies;
after which Keith climbs into his car not just to fade

but vanish with some aging bowling club girl friend
no-one guessed he had.
        With or without Mr Menzies
Tony has been stored away and Nance is telling her family:
'Let me leave Moorabbin, leave it to the Martians…'
which she does and how she ends,
tubed-up for emphysema, a granny in a granny flat,
out the back of her daughter's.

Anger Management: a South Coast Tale

If, in single motherhood there's chaos,
some days though are blessed, some days
to make you think *I like what I am seeing*
even (especially) the stubble and the sweat
this Saturday morning where,
swaying outside the supermarket, doubtless slightly stoned
he's busking.
                    And you want to talk to him,
find out where he's from and where he's staying.
Couldn't the town add more like him
to its personnel: resentful Leagues Club longtimers,
commuters, developers, the fly-in rich,
uni-bods, the tattooed, the dreadlocked, the mums
and musos.
                    And as you pay
for what's being played he slips in 'Thanks'
and how there's more this evening at the Bowlo.
        You and a girlfriend go of course.
Knowing you and what could start,
she's made damn sure you won't look plain
at all. And if not tonight (yes it's not tonight)
there's going to be one night soon, except it is
one early afternoon, a sooner-than-you-planned
and back at your place you both are talking
(talking plus the rest) well before the kids
get home.
                    And it's good getting to know him!
Somehow you feel he'll think *Nice children*
and he does. It's even better
you telling, him understanding how oh yes
their father ditched you for someone prettier,
dumber, no not ditched he's far too gentle
for that, besides he did you a service really
(most days aren't you passing the test?).
Besides they just ran off a few Ks north,
so he's reliable, their father's that
and she is too.
                    Who hasn't *baggage*?

We're adults, parents, have these relationships.
        'Relationships?' he replies. 'Good ones. Bummers.
One particularly mean bummer.'
                                And nothing's wrong
in being coy re whom he's fucked. But why?
You soon surmise what they and you possess:
lean, tanned *Been through much but gettin' my*
shit together faces, psyches still sucker for
the lesser drugs, too much drink some nights
and men, men who arriving single with a guitar
read heaps more than you do:
Hunter S. Thompson, *The Old Man and the Sea, Catch 22.*
        Surely he won't bring out jealousy and malice?
Someone though, thinking she might be a friend
needs to warn you: 'Hang loose?' she says,
'He hangs unhinged. Why'd he finish here?'
A man can't hide from what was last year's news
in certain parts of Melbourne.
Bugger any e-highway, it's that slow-marching
seep of gossip that will out,
finding such places no digit, no keyboard, no mouse
ever reaches. You and your rough diamond?
Forget the clichés.
                        But your response is *No*
it has to be. You pride yourself in knowing men,
in holding back and choosing one who mixes,
won't over-rate himself, holds the grog,
isn't a head or freak of any kind. No no no no,
he's a burley, stubbly muso in his thirties
who really likes you, whose taken to your boy
and girl with just that touch of necessary distance.
And he's moving in.

                                *

        You know he has a daughter,
but how the child is missed, that was the clincher.
Though when he talks about her he blames
not the ex, not the other ex,
but *that* ex, the Central Victorian one.

'So,' says the man, 'let's plan it.'
And getting out the map just won't relent:
down to Bateman's, up across the Monaro and the ACT,
through the Riverina, down to the Murray
and over to that vague, orchardy area round Shep,
then west to Bendigo and south where someplace
in the Goldfields they'll be, they'll have to be:
his princess and her mother the bitch.

      True that's a bit too much,
you can cope but, believing all you need
to do is calm him, and tonight's options range themselves:
certain medications, yoga, massage, massage and where
all of that might finish, and always after
you'll become that lady who can say
Yes, we'll do it, not right now of course
but one day.

       And it works.
Saturday evenings at the Bowlo you beam at
the BBQ, the mellow dope, the mums 'n' kids,
with him there swaying through his pick-up
jam sessions *Taking it from the very top*.
Why even those sour hedonists
in at the bar starring at their League
seem neutral. Nobody deals, everyone shares.
That afternoon, until you went to get
your children from their dad you both
Bet you can't…bet I can again
played dares in bed.

        Are you going to love him,
allow yourself to love him? Those friends
still trying to work it out
(warning you about him? more you about yourself!)
don't get it right.

      Sunday arvo should be even better.
In the beer garden your boy's made friends
somewhere, your girl's as ever clingy,
but happy.

       Then he joins the cover band
and during a set, whilst you're distracted,
gets annoyed, smiles of course,

but after the break he won't return
and stays annoyed.
                            What did you do?
What did you say?
                            Nothing he keeps telling
nothing. It's those pricks in the band.
Full stop. They invited him just
to make him look…well you saw
how he looked.
                            You can't tell him what
you didn't see. Which is right
and a mistake. And right. And a mistake.
            In a week you've said something and he's said
'Why'd you have to say *that* stupid?'
Then, whatever sense is left in his head
seems to swerve out in the wildest arc to hurtle back
and disintegrate.
                            You name it he throws it
(isn't *that*, it's said, what women do?).
So calm him, get him sheepish again.
With a little sweet, sexy affection
let's get him talking about himself,
ask when you can 'Why'd you do it mate?'
And loving explanations he replies it's the daughter,
he stuffed that one trusting her mother;
whilst you're relieved your god's still present,
the god of *Please never do this in front*
of my children for one day that god
mightn't be present.
                            Stoned, drunk, both or
none at all, what was he today?
Sure this afternoon you're sick of each other,
still but let's hit the Bowlo.
He smiles and sways of course, whilst you remain
too taut to flirt. Didn't he announce
'I'm a one lady man'? More than ever he is.
            He's fun, he's talented, believes you've both a future
and the kids jump into his lap. Nearing midnight
you might be listening to Chet Baker
or he's reading aloud from Neruda or

The Mersey Sound.
Then someone says something
his mind will not be clear enough to process.
They have a target, he's the target.
You better believe him, go on say it.
But this is your home and you'll say
what you like.
He won't hit you, yet;
just takes an arm, pushing it up your back
to ask 'And what about what *I'm* feeling?'
You've known him how many months
so what are you feeling? How about
Sorry mate, just don't quite get it
or more likely *Am I to blame?*
Well I never deserved this!
Or even

This isn't how you fuck.
For some nights it's still that good, he knows it is,
something has to be. And it isn't that
he's crawling back, it's worse:
he's like it hasn't happened.

*

His screaming's re-commenced. The kids are home.
And you are bruised, walking-into-a-door bruised,
like you've seen enough before except
now it's his, his bruise and possible fracture.
You saw the good man (if nobody else did)
the one who rolled you your White Ox,
the one who actually wrote songs,
the man you were loving who disguised
so much (no doubt from himself).
Well it all is out now with a sort of noise
that's heading to your kid's guts
to stay for decades. But it's when
he starts up 'Don't you get it, I love kids,
I love them!' you grab yours and lock away
the three of you, three hearts deranged
with thumping, with him outside the toilet
howling, whilst you phone your girlfriends.

Men arrive, and now he screams at them:
the Bowlo band, the cover band, the busking partner
who then reaches for what you never thought
you'd reach with him: cops, their AVOs.
Oh, and you're reasoning again,
he was never thick, some cops are truly thick
and sometimes we need what the thick provide.
      Meantime he'll be off,
a stocky, perspiring man, making noises no one wants
to understand, getting dragged away.

                  *

      Blue-eyed handsome, by-the-book neutral,
with blonde hair in regulation buns,
when the women mention you by name,
that name he cried every time (you're fearing now)
he loved you *They're on my side*
you start to think *they have to be.*
      You say: 'Domestics must be
your very worst, right?'
                  They say:
'Shall we send for the children's father?'
And you have to ask for a repeat,
you can't quite get what they've said.
      They point to your face:
how will you get this attended to?
      You have the answer:
your best friend in the area's a nurse.
      You want to stay indoors? You'll stay indoors
for days because you've planned enough,
you've planned too hard.
This could've worked except he's sick
and stupid. *Once is a shock,*
twice you're a failure, but three times
that's a pattern and three times mate,
matey, sport and Sonny Jim you're out.
Oh by the way that was Number Three.
Hadn't grief disposed of your bravado
you might've said it.

Whilst you locked yourself away
the Bowlo's kicked all hippies out.
By now it's spring. Whatever's replaced League
the sullen bar is staring at it.
They may be grubby, certainly are trash, but none's
as violent as he is; and if you hear *Closure*
once again you'll snap anything in half,
knowing this sound's simpler:
He's off to find another fool.

The women cops arrange their closure
but he doesn't make a time to apologize
he makes a time to explain.
Some might say *Get into anger management mate,*
right into it whilst others sneer
You are a weak, weak man.

You though make a time to hardly listen,
just to be assured they're heading off now:
sheepish him, his reading matter and guitar
through regional Australia.

Waitin' for the Viet Cong

The speaker is a recently retired femocrat.

...in this way my mother, my late mother told it:
how their elder daughter, scholarship holder/doctoral candidate,
had disappeared and how that winter in Paris,
as chill turned flu turned pleurisy turned pneumonia
no-one, not even her parents let alone those friends
The Collective, knew her whereabouts:
that had all stopped where and when a sad girl left
without her forwarding address.
                              But as if my dad decreed
She's our rebel and nobody else's
I was to be saved in a way most never could be saved,
by an establishment finding its own
and bringing her home.
                         'Just a few days short of death,
that's right of death...' my mother told it,
'but we set to work we did, yes everybody did
to find and save her.'
                      She mightn't have composed
this saga of a family's miracle, she sure was its conductor though;
and if I still defer to certain of its merits
here's the exception: this tale she told
(eyes wide alight in their bewildered pride)
was hers, and hardly mine: the girl,
so well past crying now, who having had some breakdown
was back home with her parents.

                         *

       If only she'd never *meant* it!
Did that woman really announce (and yes she did):
'I'd like you all to meet our elder daughter, the brilliant Marxist-Leninist...'?
What kind of La Mama farce was this?
For there would be my mama, this fifty year old high school librarian
trundling out to friends her Great Story: when all I wanted
was to regale her with mine: be-dumped or dump.
       There is that moment when,

no matter her age a child needs to announce
Yes, yours was my upbringing, nobody else did it,
but you will never understand now, will you?

    And *Understand? We do we do* came their stammering chorus
of concern: parents, educators, clerics, whoever was in vogue
But but what of your future?

*

    When I still lived with my folks I might bring
The Collective home: these were my people, people ablaze
with all that kind of courage History supplies:
every argument good as won. 'Good afternoon Professor,
meet the vanguard who'll be taking over.'
    Isn't there a perverse fun
meeting those you'd love to see purged?
For on occasions Dad might take my sister and myself
to the Staff Club, as if to teach
This is no 'other half', this is 'our half',
see how we live?
        Then, as they glanced my way
how I enjoyed imagining the Staff Club's condescensions:
What are *we going to do with them:*
our angry children and their amazing brains?
    Not all of us. Someone from a milder faction
kept courting my sister; when she turned twenty,
he told his mother they would live together
(who shrieked then ordered them married).
    Now there was a pair so willing to facilitate 'dialogue',
any 'dialogue' with any one,
a couple whose future was that much in the present
it seemed near enough the past; whilst mine
just hoped the greater stories might commence:
all those things we'd live to see happen, happening:
getting rid of Imperialism for starters,
after which anything bourgeois.
    I was so adept at *bourgeois* wasn't I,
using the whole Collective-at-its-grandest-heights'
greatest label of abuse (even if that's what we were, bourgeois).
Sometimes I fear these were the last occasions it was ever

employed; the saddest fact, for what other word remotely evoked
our world, that world we needed to replace?

But for all his loving pragmatism *Lies?*
I wish now I could have told my dad the professor
I can accept living lies, but we've been living games!
With *we* being our family or The Collective or just
me and the girl I'd been loving near a decade.

And she was Antoinette.

*

When my sister and I were still in high school
Dad took his family on sabbatical.
And in the girl's school adjacent to the Red Brick
(its chaffing pettinesses, those scandalous inevitables)
you might say I wanted to leave, immediately leave
except for where? What puritan like me would need
the vapid joys of Swinging London? Besides,
the Sister School, the French girls had arrived
and if I was distracted now, I was ah-so-anchored!

This was Antoinette and I:
some enchanted evening you may see this someone
you'll wish to see again, again, again, then
fly to my side and guessing I'll understand ask
*Where exactly are you from and what exactly
do they do there?*

From then who needed any bourgeoisie,
when each was such an aristocrat for the other?
Ours always would remain an aristocrat's revolt,
the skewed truth matched by the necessary swagger.

Thin like me without my bumps and angles
Antoinette was lithe, that gamin type made for barricades,
with her well-aimed assassin of a mind designed
so that Imperialism would be hacked and hacked
to what it always was: a big-noting fraud for
men with connections.

She'd come to stay,
I'd go to stay, at sixteen I'd the best indeed the only
kind of friend I needed; and on some nights
(it felt like I could never stop)

just speaking French and French again!
                                        'Yes, the French girl...'
Mother never asked so much as alluded:
something you knew she knew just wasn't jelling.
What though? Antoinette may not have been polite
she sure was diplomatic though.
This she seemed to deliver, is how we'll deal
with *them*. Well at least my dad,
who'd see me to or meet me at the boat train.
          And I recall (could I ever not?)
how Antoinette took me some place where women,
women were looking at each other and it all seemed
a matter of love. Till then I'd hardly thought like that
(she knew I hadn't) but something was making sense
and making even more sense
whenever we kissed.
                        Whilst in a room stuffy from a low fire
and his perspiration, I met her sad-eyed, chain-smoking
Stalinist father, who told us what we already guessed,
and guessing knew: that all the world which really mattered
were disposing now, right now with empires.
          Three, four, five times in six months
she and I met, loved, separated and cried
(and I was not that kind of girl to cry).
Now sabbatical over, our family was returning
and with another empire poised for its disposal,
the only world I wanted known was waiting,
waiting for Viet Cong.

                            *

          When mother uncovered I was 'on the pill'
(a term that dates both cause and its reaction)
our grand implosion arrived.
                        'Couldn't you,
couldn't you...' she sure had gagged on something,
'just...just...protect yourself?'
                        With what?
Whilst these I still assume are what had hurt:
she never knew I'd been to see a doctor

and that shuddering idea some stupid boy
might find her potential University Medallist attractive,
or failing that easy. Meanwhile she,
the once so ever-worldly and aware,
turned into the silliest woman I would ever know
(except of course myself).
      It helped she was a fool:
though I needn't worry about that need I,
since weren't there mightier concerns?
                        When Paris
seemed like it had been shot out of France into
and beyond the heavens, I knew the time was mine,
was ours.
        Air-mailing Antoinette,
near frying myself with jealousy at their struggles,
how they were leading the world where the world
just had to be led, whilst here I was
attempting a collective life in back street suburbia:
girls like me, lean, spectacled correct-liners,
or the dumpy ones, jolly and spread out in their jeans;
those impossibly deep-voiced boys,
or the frizzy-haired ones forever quoting Dylan
in Dylan voices as if they'd truly written the stuff;
and runaways who'd finish running on or running back;
all of it banal, ludicrous, remarkable, so that you
would wake to another day of your revolt thinking
This is beautiful for this is History
and if there's to be a vanguard, guess what, it's us,
for we are going to truly matter
and I am going to return to Antoinette.

           *

      Nothing I would ever do had been so planned,
so mis-planned.
        Candidacy and scholarship were certainties
whilst French would never be a problem:
wasn't it all mine, not as a kind of loan
but the zealous gift which, steeled and committed,
I thought had chosen me, such being that on-cue bravado

History and love both offer.
                              Shy, arrogant girls,
hadn't we kept each other's photographs
'Moi sur Les Barricades', 'Me and my Collective'?
Maybe. But what hers had hardly shown
was all the ground she'd filled, she'd travelled,
which wasn't, I kne,w mere breasts and a boyfriend.
Much worse she couldn't, wouldn't announce
Don't you understand, we're hardly like that now!
            Like any liberation I needed a future.
Well here came my future folding into its present
and then refolding into its past, with Antoinette asking
'Haven't you had boys?'
                        I had my answer
to a different question: 'Aren't I on the pill?'
(That something to make girls comfortable and annoy mothers.)
            Then catching this right-through-me look of hers
I knew what she was seeing *Here's that Australiene again*
(some place like that) a pest from my past,
and how right now in the compost of our caprice
and paranoia, my Antoinette was truly blooming.
Who did she think we had been?
Just two young women sending aerograms
and she was probably correct. Best be bland best say
She cut me and I caught a chill
as I'd say now except all I could taste
(all I wanted to taste) were vinegar tears;
as all I believed turned pleurisy and beyond.
            In some grubby bed I lay, devastated yet proud:
At least I'm bad this *bad! Could there be a better way to die?*
With little else to appreciate, why not revel in that?

                              *

            Since they were after me, those who thought they understood;
though nowadays I'd simply say her fellow bourgeoisie
were tracking down a very sick Australian girl,
of whom they'd later say was somehow saved
by telegrams, cablegrams (they meant a lot in those days
telegrams, cablegrams) and an embassy's footwork.

Week after shaky week I'd little else but sweated,
though now someone was saying my name and I caught that
monotonal national voice diplomacy never could dispel.
Whilst all those manner of people I wished exterminated:
governments, Foreign Affairs, specialists, flight crew, anyone
wanting the world purged of every Antoinette-and-I
were helping to lift, mend, fly and propel me
through Customs and out, school girl ruthless still.
As if that mattered for, whatever my posture
I was only posture now: graceful, graceless, remorseful,
remorseless. O you dumb and greedy little monster!

*

'You realise,' my sister and her spouse confided,
'it was their networks found you...' itemising
some of my most abhorred Staff Club names.
But as with Antoinette the only 'catch' was irony;
when Dad thanked them on my behalf and all turned History,
unalterable History.

*

The Collective was dissolving as what replaced it
made their own mistakes re-making ours.
I tutored then I stopped to start a new life:
policy/consultancy/policy/consultancy.
I loved somebody, I loved somebody else.
I put aside telling Mother of 'Antoinette the Sequel'
but then she died. Dad remarried so I told them,
humanism all the way.
                    'That was love.'
In the movie he'd have intoned these words
deep in a mellow book-lined den.
But being on the patio of their townhouse
he had to laugh. 'Love. It can't have been much else.
And you always were whatever you always were.'
            'Taa Dad.' Then I laughed too.

*

We knew Struggle, we knew Truth,
        Knew Hué and Hai Phong,
Served such causes in our youth,
        Waitin' for the Viet Cong.
Whilst Johnson, Nixon straffed the North,
Bellowed each July the Fourth:
"Longin' for the Viet Cong to win girls,
        Screamin' for the Viet Cong!"

[They grew, the thick red arrows grew,
        Each downward swelling prong
(Courtesy of Fu Manchu)
        Waitin' for the Viet Cong:
With ev'ry Indo-Chinese peasant
Craving his slice of Karinya Crescent,
Slaughter us the Viet Cong sure will, boys…
        Better kill the Viet Cong!]

One Sunday circa ten to five
        Hearing our door bell's gong:
From parents on some arvo drive
        (Waitin' for the Viet Cong).
Did they clang forth 'The East Is Red'
Those chimes which shot us out of bed?
At home with the Viet Cong, 'Hi Oldies!'
        'It's a pleasure, Viet Cong.'

Some played Dylan, some played Ochs,
        And others Cheech and Chong.
Whilst some just played at (said their folks)
        Waitin' for the Viet Cong.
With visions packed within each spliff
Like scenes from 'Blow Up', 'MASH' and 'If…'
Somethin' for the Viet Cong? Oh save us,
        Nothin' like the Viet Cong!

My sister married blissed on grass,
        She wore a sarong.
(I near-to-almost missed that farce
        Waitin' for the Viet Cong.)

Later, back at their bourgeois ranch
Where her spouse ran his Labor Party branch,
'Why wait for the Viet Cong?' I'd taunt. 'I'm
    Wedded to the Viet Cong!'

Innocent women innocent men
    Little we did seems wrong.
A stroll to the shops then home again
    (Waitin' for the Viet Cong).
Went abroad copped much the same.
'Now what,' she asked me 'is your name?'
Sobbin' for the Viet Cong (boo hoo hoo)
    Howlin' for the Viet Cong!

Operation Hendrickson

for Ben Michell

and he told the truth, mainly.
        Huckleberry Finn

1 Carnival Knowledge Blues

b4i\ uru
        16
An old equation

   Okay, she was fifteen. And here's the new equation,
their real equation: either she's sixteen or isn't.
Sure wasn't.
      But *moral danger*? Behind me she held on and
after that all we mostly did was ride and talk
(anyone thought I might look after her?)
just ride and talk.
     Well now let's mention it:
how someone was knocking at my door who sure wasn't
Barnacle Bill. Oh what could I, Henn in Little Kim's sarong
possibly offer these jacks with all their *Operation Hendrickson*
all their *Going Asian, Bob?* A song?
My *Carnival Knowledge Blues*?
        'Look, look, at it again,
twenty years old and still can't learn his limits.
Hardly civilised, Bob,' they giggled to themselves,
arranging such evidence to send a magistrate into
bored, impatient sighs, end up in some local rag
to show the mates, and really thrill the Old Girl
who wasn't denying anything and didn't have to,
not when she was set on praying for me to God,
her *You'll keep* God.
     How'd you'd ever finish here?
I'd a few days to ask and wait the answer out.
   Till finally in court I'm seeing Hannaford,
Wes Hannaford, working for *them.*
(Apart from where we were, we could've had one glorious

What the…? double-take routine.) Later of course,
when he gets to visit the cells, he's told
'Sure I did it but I'm innocent, right?'
Whilst Wes just stares some *Really?* squarehead stare.

*

They're dragging my girl to Winlaton
To make her a virgin again,
Lezzo screws will protect her
From alcohol, hormones and men.

I'm in need of, its reckoned, reforming
With sessions of backs-to-the-wall.
Well I've learnt this from carnival knowledge,
Love's rated at sweet bugger-all.

2 The Large House in Lalwa Street

When I was twelve Kildonan closed their Canterbury place,
so we headed five or six miles east.
Foster care was moving out of 'homes'
and into houses, houses with folks, kids
or those like me who'd been long adopted.
My Old Girl used to say how the church
(and always it seemed to be the church)
wanted to move into the more modern world,
which in our case was a house, one like any other,
if a bit larger to hold its ever-constant foster family.
And this was me then: *You there! Him!*
The one always getting the joke too quick,
much too quick! Introducing Henn,
him wanting to get there hours in front of anyone,
him who even then when he thought 'bikes', never meant
the pedal kind.
Always looking about myself,
if hardly at myself.
And when I found love, or thought I did,
I liked it.

I could be many people's boy,
which still is now advantage/disadvantage;
for it can remain such a bewildering comfort,
guessing how much you'll never know (especially about yourself).
Which to my Old Girl meant God,
God plus the large house in Lalwa Street.

                                       Which was our template.
The mixture though might be rather different.

3 Proper Gander

        When it's *Hot dog!* time, when there's been some
Rumble at the youth club and *Yeah man yeah it's the bodgies!*
you know that's Atchison even beyond himself,
all too lame to be pathetic (or might that be reversed?)
If we're bothered we try finding time to whine
'Lay off Atchison…' but hardly end the sentence.
        Meanwhile 'Pinky' Rushworth giggles
in his 'Pinky' way, Patterson's talkin' American
from the side of his mouth (or is it his head?)
and when I ask Nam what 'nam' means in Chinese
I'm told 'backward man'. So I guess it does.
        When Degan at thirteen wants to leave
and join the Navy, I'm ready to believe him.
        Who though wants to believe McKibbon? No one.
        Whilst Wearney you needn't believe because
he's just making it up for *Proper Gander*,
his rag: 'Hey Wearney, write my memoirs
then put them into your *Proper Gander*!'
In our concert he plays the butler,
who sees it (and I mean it) all.
                    Then Cruikshank takes
one half of the curtain, I take the other and
at the end of every act we're rushing it across.
I like that.
        Armitage believing he's a beatnik
founds the Royal Australian Beatnik Society,
and, lifting items from *Mad* passes them for his own.
He tells me only poofters play with girls.

So I don't. My loss.

4 Up on the Roof

      Let's see. It's lunchtime and someone prowls the roof,
our high school roof. And that's not me up there.
I'm watching, I'm cheering as the school is watching,
cheering somebody we hardly know prancing like
he's Top Forty material *Come up and get me!*
Come up and get me!
                      You think it can be explained
how *He's adopted, she's in foster care?*
That won't 'explain'. You'll never know
what to do with us and never will
-Robert, Royce, Debra, Linda, Phil-
that two that five percent in cottages and homes.
      Well whoever she is my mother runs a tuckshop,
serves behind a counter at Coles, something simple now
for the most normal lady in the world
(which is how I want her). And who *he* was
my father, I like convincing myself,
was at best an admirable lair,
a someone up on the roof, not me and that's about it.
      Quite soon I will do dumber things
but that lunch hour I don't have so much
to prove (never was a performer)
as forth, pirouette back and do it again
he's enjoying what he thinks heroes enjoy
You'll talk about all this for years. Oh sure.
But not in the way you want it talked.

5 Punchlines

Lew-Fatt deserves some TV show;
Kidder's a trainee thug;
for a fine-tuned tongue and a fine-tuned slap
can play you for their mug.

Half past twelve, here comes the choice:
to giggle or be whacked,
in a yard entranced by this Phil 'n' Bob
lunchtime double act.

Kidder steps back and staring smirks.
His little mate meanwhile
digs with a neh-neh *to the ribs*
Lou (that's Costello) style.

It's a boys-stuff world with two who seem
our resident Mafiosi
(so best keep your noses far from this
Jillian, Janice, Josie)

though when quite soon all turns to sport
(here comes the 'sorry' stuff)
they've caught on smart to that grown-up art:
how far seems far enough.

Brats with brains who reckon they know
just where their mayhem stops.
Trust one? Trust none? We'll leave it there,
thanking they aren't the cops.

6 Caveman

      I know enough of God to know God knows when he's been had;
or when God's bored, so bored with certain pious stunts
he just gives in. There's even times when all God sees
is full collapse and walks away.
                                With his long, block of a face
the Old Man looked like Thor, whilst heaven
for my Old Girl became her special kind of milk bar:
some might get served, most certainly wouldn't.
      Our minister (when it wasn't time for preaching)
wore polo necks and cords. He had two sons.
The older, quiet one stared a lot and did his homework.
Caveman was his brother.

Some of us (not me I hope)
can only live with full disturbance, whilst some of these
don't even want to guess what happens next.
And after them (after God has seen it all in full collapse)
Caveman enters, Caveman is taking over:
not Taylor who only picked our softer targets,
not Kidder with all his easy time to tune
his low key menace, not smart-arse and truly pushing it
as Lew-Fatt did, but Caveman, our one boy
Panzer Division.
                    So you might walk past a classroom
(and you made certain you did) just to see him,
our minister's twelve-year-old throwing chairs,
lots of them (and what was the rumour…he threw one at
a girl?). You sure could get an easy rise from Caveman,
and watch him turn, turn into Caveman Plus.
Watching him: isn't that what Gods and boys do well?
Though it was no minister's corduroy God,
but that deeper other God, the one greeting you when born:
'Like to meet the World, Caveman, like to meet
the Caveman, World?'
                    And wasn't it all like
some smug, very new teacher who announces
'So, you're our famous Caveman?' someone
(let's try calling him God) making you his special joke,
making sure you have to live and wear that joke forever.
        Now ya gotta remember this one!
This what? This *Spartacus* matinee when Kirk Douglas
wraps his toga around Jean Simmons
and an entire Morton Park Hall erupts with absolute certainty
of what they're seeing. Well it's then, piping above the mayhem
that Caveman contributes 'Touché away! Touché away!'
his Caveman war cry. Which is when,
someone, doubtless God again, has had enough
and belts him on the nose.
            Which is not the end but the beginning.
By now Caveman's on stage and, wanting to star in *Spartacus*
he grabs the screen and is pulling Kirk Douglas, Tony Curtis,
an entire Hollywood down to the floor.
And here is what we may as well be hearing:

'Look at me, admire what I can cause,
for if you cannot trust what happens next *you'll* happen next,
there's no-one else when Caveman is in charge!'
   Getting older, and I was getting older,
you soon learnt the labelling: dislocated, tragic,
one total boring pill. Or if you were younger
and one of his few, few approximate friends,
you soon learnt to take after God, your God that is,
the one who walks away.

7 In Johnny's Kitchen

   This is the news. Firstly I wasn't quite the news,
not then, not for Wearney's *Proper Gander* news,
not like those, Atchison for one, Wearney
loved annoying.
     'Don't bug me do you dig it man?'
Atchison proclaimed, never realising just how well
Atchison was being dug.
     But Wearney,
if you're wanting news come round to my place
where, behind her kitchen bench:
'This is the news read by Old Girl Hendrickson...
We do it this way, not *their* way but
our way. Why? Because we're special.
Translation: do what you're told...'
With a smile as big as her tits, an adopter,
a foster mum, a negotiator, a forgiver,
but God's ever-resident two-i-c.
     So I'll give a list,
a list of names for the news:
Johnny, Hannaford, me, someone else and Johnny's chick.
Not only did we never get there,
we hardly even started never-getting-there.
We'd been sent where we'd been sent
because it wasn't the Tech. I'll say it wasn't.
By now it wasn't anything.
And doing the place a service we simply wagged
that morning.

Drugs? No drugs in those days.
In Johnny's parent's kitchen it was
pancakes all the way.
                    Till somehow they're told,
and Miller and Knight (headmaster/senior master)
both in their suits of shiny-grey are hammering
on Johnny's parent's door, like they're the FBI.
            And now we're the news, we've a decade's news!
            In front of an entire school Johnny apologises
(for what no-one's exactly sure) goes loony during Nasho,
then loonier in Lilydale; I meanwhile
jump over his back fence into, I love to think,
a paddock shoulder high with great, weird,
Nepalese shit; working at the brickworks
Hannaford saves for three years to sail the globe,
returning he turns squarehead;
they forgot about the other guy (why was he ever there?)
but the last time I saw him he was into
Chariot of the Gods? truly believing it;
and Johnny's chick got sent to Chick's Tech,
smart move, their very smartest.

8 Taylor

            His words gone out, he's set to pull
the tough cunt act.
                    I'm there that night
when Taylor turns deranged inside the Dragon Palace.
Less than sweet, more than a touch sour,
we're set for fun, to watch somebody rise,
and he will, though not how he's required.
            We're all there: those who've caught the rumour,
those trailing after Taylor; those seduced
by how events can push themselves.
Though no friends to announce *Leave it Taylor.*
Taylor won't have them, just allies, acquaintances,
those he'll meet in pubs.
                    But revenge-for-something's on
and out it pours: on edge then getting louder

Taylor stares, demands and threatens.

Till Mr Dragon, in his high-pitched grasp of English
screams: 'I call my boys, I call police!
I call you fuckwit Taylor call you poofter!'
Which is the last he'll call until tomorrow.

And if you think that's where Taylor stops,
it's where he starts.
For if he's slight and lean that means
speed and muscle. Table to table he strides
hurling the bowls and plates, howling all his
Slants 'n' slopes 'n' go-back-where-y'-came-froms.
He wants applause. But everyone's too stunned to give it.
And, as he strides past I look and know
If I could hate that *much Taylor, I never would.*
So I don't.

'I'm no friend of any jack,'
a rough, smart voice announces. 'But they can have him.
Come on come on, look at my face,
let's have some perspective. Guess who's part Chink?'
For Lew-Fatt's there. Lew-Fatt's always there.
Lew-Fatt says: 'I must be getting old.
I know what the limits are.' And we agree.

(Still, he could tell the vilest jokes
Lew-Fatt do you have to? ever heard.
'There was this ugly pro, see…'
you bet there was, and thinking of it
still settles in me like something I never
should've eaten.)

But with Taylor gone
Lew-Fatt's sneering. And there's little beats
a twisted teenage sneer to guess at things
we never were allowed to guess
(Lew-Fatt's been made to survive like that).

'Sometime tonight,' we're told,
'but when he's alone Taylor will be in tears.
Can you imagine it? Taylor in tears!
Anyone staying around for the jacks…
what, no volunteers?

9 The 'Johnny's got called up and is going into the army' Party
Song

They hold it at his girlfriend's parents:
sun-deck, patio and pool,
chicks down one end 'round an ashtray
puffin' Alpine, puffin' Kool.

When I rev up the father's drinking
in his garage, on a stool.
'Heard you comin' half an hour back,
next time why not try a mule?'

Funny bastard. Then: 'You know him,
fiancé of my family jewel?'
And itemises all those who'll keep:
'You 'n' you 'n' you 'n' you'll...'

Mirror ball with daggy patterns,
music with its woo-woo-woo'll.
(Glanced about me, not one Elvis,
'Love Me Tender', 'Don't Be Cruel'.)

Johnny's maudlin (I hate maudlin)
like he's an apprentice ghoul,
but since the party's his, he's breaking
each written and unwritten rule:

after hours still churning, churning
thoughts like they are on some spool:
these it seems are his essentials:
y'mates, y'head, y'heart, y'tool.

Leaving few doubts what he'll take on
(authorities to make him drool)
silly ass Pom (as in Boy Scouts)
officers like 'Sir' at school.

With a cringing 'Bye bye Johnny...'
(hypocrisy sure ain't my fuel)

'there's this other party…' (isn't)
which excuse ran thin as gruel.

I bewildered sigh 'It's tragic
when a mate unfolds as fool.'
Turn bemused though, throttle westward:
I won't stop till Warrnambool.

10 The Nasho of Love

           All very well
The Mission of Saint James and Saint John
and all its deaconesses feeling concerned
for Little Kim and her deadshit folks.
           Me and my concern though,
we thanked them and their concern.
And then I asked her what she'd like to do.
           Of course I took her riding,
that riding which finished us hot.
Hot and shivering.
                    Bye-bye
to all our *will or won't we* show,
no way we wouldn't.
                    Plenty soon
everything was -as only a girl can say it-
'Growly!'
           And, as only a boy replies:
'Growly-plus with added Henn!'
she understood.
           So,
what were we going to tell her deaconesses?
           'Lookee here, I'm no lord 'n' saviour,
deaconesses. Though you tell me who is?
I just want to look after Little Kim.'
           Oh yeah?

                    *

In Box Hill around that time
I ran into Fatty Hosking in a bus shelter:
sixteen, seventeen tops, some mad bitch
who no way would be seventeen tops again,
spread all over his knees, smoochin'.
      What man could get away with *that*?
The way no man could get away with telling me
(me whom she had never met before)
how good and she meant *good* her Fatty was.
      'No way,' I laughed, 'no way. No way eh?
How long you two known each other?'
      'Three weeks,' she skited in her yuck-yuck way.
      Why blame her? Mightn't this be love?
Well done.

*

      Last year, down the City's western end,
recognizing Fatty (who might or mightn't know
just who I am) I get told how he worked as a boner,
as a slaughterman etcetera,
out past Brooklyn; slept at Markillies
and other flop palaces.
      With the love, the good love of drink
getting him through the boning and the slaughtering
(he stank of all three) no way would I remind him how
last time we met, he was hosting on his knees
some shrieker woman, in a bus shelter;
maybe the best thing ever in his life.

*

      And who needs these reminders:
You were a dickhead then,
you are a dickhead now
or *Isn't it sure fabulous*
the way your patterns kick in?
      If some were set (their bad luck)
for Nasho, I'd be set for mine
i.e. the Nasho of Love:

Sergeant-Major Henn pronouncing:
'Today, worms, I'll be showing youse
both how to use it and how to make this world's
Little Kims extremely happy.'
                              Not likely.
It'd be me trying to tell them,
those jacks and deaconesses: 'Fellas, fellas,
she's older than she looks. True.
And it wasn't us public-smoochin' in some bus shelter,
Kim left what wasn't quite a home to prop with me
where I was rooming.'
          No way of course, no conceivable way.
          So who needs reminders now,
from those reckoning you're still
their special, veteran kind of novelty rooter?
          'You're Henn,' they'll quiz.
'weren't you done for Carnival Knowledge?'
          Done once I wish I could remind them
though I don't, *done once for love.*

11 Johnny's Great Escape

          Pumped-up for his war Johnny went on about noise:
the tanks (there were tanks weren't there?) the rockets
(rockets surely) the guns, guns and our damn good reason
Either we are there or they are here.
And if he were caught (VCs or MPs
name him the difference, this war would be his!)
if he were caught, wouldn't it be all *vroom-vroom*
like Steve McQueen in *The Great Escape*?
So I supposed that *vroom* was how war sounds.
But they were sending *him* to an actual war?

                    *

          Horrified he'd ever been to war, this Johnny
came marching home to Lilydale, acid and a pension.
One arvo in some street we saw each other, and I heard:
'I was just thinking of you. And there you are.'

              'Like that?'
                        'Like that.'
                                  'Good stuff?'
                                            'Not bad…'
and we went back to his place:
bare floors, bare walls, one two three four…
ten pieces of furniture max!
No Asian trophies, no snaps of the lads, just echoes
plus a yard to walk around in.
Missus and kids, somewhere.)

                        *

          He gave me one small tab and that night
I was walking north where Punt Road overpasses
Dandenong Road at St Kilda Junction,
pushing myself into the warm October air
as it kept folding around me. I was so pleased,
nothing would stall wherever I went.

12 Meanwhile, Elsewhere…

          'Now Robert,' they would have to ask,
well-meaning, more naïve
than I could ever be, 'now Robert,
what would you like to do?
You know, with your *life*?'
          They couldn't understand,
I couldn't understand how there'd be
no idea.
          For you had to be adult,
we'll call it that, to grasp that almighty
how-it-was-approximate-heaven
to cruise one side of Patpong Road
then back up the other, all speedy-mellow,
waiting for Crazy Horse to open,
giving the FucFuc trannies
your bemused check-out, your
widest berth.

Was it that town,
was it any town (after all
it's what I might imagine occurring)
where I landed in some hotel lobby,
next to a retired teacher
(sixty-six she told me)
who flicking a hand the local's way
announced: 'They're coming all right,
coming right down and who's
to blame 'em?'
            Right now of course
they didn't seem to be, besides
I was heading their way,
heading as much as Johnny had been
if for differing results.
            I was an alien on Alien Tours,
smoking something with tribesmen
(how'd they ever get much done...
well they probably didn't)
when my blessed twelve-hour lock-jaw
arrived, held me and departed;
burping once, for eternity I reckon,
which entertained the tribesmen.
            And when they want us to leave,
there'll be no way we won't.
            And if you think all this
will last, oh yes it will, if you are dead.
            But till then *Robert,*
what would you really *like to do?*

13 Walkin' Away

            At Bowater-Scott's four-to-midnight shift,
where you could lick the tang from all those
hefty-enormous tubes of pulp,
some goose proclaimed: 'If chicks bleed then
chicks are ready.'
            Get caught, I considered answering
but didn't. *Get caught Goose and whilst you're about it*

fall in love. If she won't break your heart
(what heart?) the Vice Squad's sure to break
your balls ha ha and there she goes Goose
walkin' away, she's walkin' away...

                                    And yet
the number of nights I've ended with this girl
and oops you're at it again, didn't think
that was bound to happen but it did.

        I was twenty-six and thought I'd like to be French.
When you're French you just say
Hi, I'm Monsieur Henn, cherie. And being French
you're always ready to risk it for a face and what a face!
always ready to see that risk and know it's yours.

        Tell you what monsieur, there's girls and real girls.
Go and announce to a real girl *Wow, you're gorgeous!*
and see where you land, you both land.

14 Tait

Tait had gone to Burwood Tech
might've got a trade,
if a girl was so inclined
possibly got laid.

Slightly brightish it's recalled,
just this side of perplexed.
I've little idea what happened though
next 'n' next 'n' next,

till I couldn't miss his face
front page of The Sun
with Tait the very centre of
victim-centred fun.

Who got pushed by trashy clowns
each with his trashy grin,
from South Yarra station
just as a train rolled in.

Don't wish to know that venom which
drive 'em to see Tait dead
(was he some kind of poofter?
anything he said?).

I want to know that pinpoint though
vengeance rests upon:
Tait's God had second-guessed them,
he hahaha lived on.

'Weren't my fault,' each maintained
with manufactured fury.
Deadshits thinking the court contained
a deadshit judge and jury,

thought they'd play the jargon card
(a.k.a. baloney)
blaming it on that Mafia boss
Don Testosteroné.

Blaming it all on headaches
out their excuses puffed.
And oh God's sure an ironic God
for like 'em Tait was stuffed.

Beanie'd, drool'd, track-suited,
one-eyed, dressing-gowned,
through all of his remaining life
snarling, wheel-chair bound.

I can't come up with clever words.
I'm boiling 'em down to 'hate'.
Name one sounding plainer, better.
End of Bobby Tait.

15 Amateurs

I think I recall them, may have met them,
seen them once, anyway I heard about this couple
(when it's a couple a lot is set to turn tragic)
who brought in stuff for some other crowd
except, except, wanting first taste it's
boom! through customs *boom!* in the taxi *boom!*
to their lounge room and I mean,
with all their thumping hearts and frigging *boom!*
why try it? Oh but they tried it and there they lay
both in matching pairs of King Gee overalls
and do not ask me or anybody why. Amateurs.

*

Or there was big Col Bird
who lived in the next street,
called everybody's mother Mrs
(but then we all did)
who had this joke:
'Beg pardon Mrs but swearin' –
it's me fuckin' hobby!'
Well everybody has a hobby,
starting out. He had a few,
we all did. But on it off it
on it again, there he was
still calling it a 'hobby'?
One more amateur. (Some place
I'm told, at the end of the Alamein Line.)

16 The Hendricksons

Old Man Hendrickson was indeed an old man,
the kind who understood just too damn much i.e.
If he had got away with it his son would not.
Why say much else? He didn't have to.
The man ignored Hannaford, thought Johnny contemptible
and when Wearney tried talking with him, dumb try Wearney.

But with his wild sweep of silver brush-back hair and unbreakable
Viking jaw, I rather liked this quiet, consistent man.
       After he sat down in his shed and died, my Old Girl,
his widow moved in with one of her sisters, on the Peninsula.
They prepared a sleep-out for me and once a month or twice
if Robert were in the country he might prop there.
Via all that prayer and worry had she somehow anchored me?
She thought so and for a while, a small while, might have.
Except I wrote a poem.

A Poem in Two Parts

I've been to Nepal
seen it all

seen it all
I've been to Nepal

       And you need never know it Mum
but
that
means
what
it
means.

17 Henn's Day

       Walk right in, sit right down,
it's Henn's day.
           Good morning. Let's be introduced.
You've heard of victimless crime, right?
Well meet the original victimless criminal:
me. And if you mean you don't 'do drugs',
you've just never met the right drug.
                Good afternoon.
Then there were those days they tried convincing us
sure were *the best ever*. Plus, wait for it,
there would be *more*. Well here's the more:

a fissure ripped through everybody's life
and it all stopped, if indeed it started.

      The disappointments that bring on the big-noting,
the anger when the big-note's not accepted,
having to cope with their tiny place in the world,
the world of sour men I've never wished to live in
though I've had to, each day a further round of
squaring off, shake hands, square off again.

                              Good evening.
I'm thirty-one and old enough to announce: 'No perspective,
we never had any fuckin' perspective!'
And if Johnny got a war for his perspective,
some perspective: sitting in Lilydale
till the time arrives to get up, take a walk,
return and phone the dealer.

                           'Good stuff?'

                              'Not bad.'

18 Pole-axed

      So you're driving past some church,
a weekday, seeing these kids outside,
kids who've hardly been to church,
kids who've assembled very very swiftly
and you know it: they're mourning that man
who pole-axed total no-one but himself,
some place out past Stud Road.

      Which seems ridiculous since
Kidder always took his time;
and you wouldn't want to cop Kidder
waiting, merely waiting, the only one to know
what he would do, which wasn't of course charm
but sure made Kidder, once.

      Whilst here he is, the man in charge of
the world's foulest jokes, Lew-Fatt saying
'Top man, top man…' and
'Kidder was supposed to take his time…'
Though it isn't tears Lew-Fatt fears
but those all-too-many questions that

everyone stares at or better/worse wishes
to avoid.

       Too much Bob Kidder
is far too much for Phil Lew-Fatt,
and of course he's snappy now, waving his arms
at people he knows or recognises,
or doesn't want to recognise or know.

       'What do you think it is it is, this life this life?
Some bright elusive butterfly of love?'

19 Caveman 2

       Don't mean to be in the area but I am.
       And he doesn't know me (hardly needs to know anyone)
but at 'The Chase' or whatever it is being called,
there he is, Caveman (his Caveman gene having moved into its next,
drearier phase) stacking trolleys as they come wheeling off
the escalators.
       And here's what I won't be asking:
Do you know we used to walk past your classroom,
just to see you in action, and wasn't there that time
you threw chairs at a girl? Didn't you know
how everyone went bug-eyed at you,
and did you ever mind? Is God still trying to break you,
and how many times have you been broken, anyway?
       Whilst here is what he never will reply:
Maybe maybe, sort of sort of, not my God, not many
hardly any none.
       And I'm thinking of his brother,
the minister's other son who stayed with his homework
and just kept staring.
       Oh Caveman,
if I'd you for a brother I'd have sure done my homework,
all my homework.

20 That's what it's all about

   ...and if it's heading a decade since those few,
hardly memorable Carnival Knowledge months,
how are we rating this-best-home-grown-that's-ever-been-rolled
1978?
  Tell you what::
coming out of the bank and that man's
Wearney.
   'G'day Wearney...
been meaning to ask you:
which of us at school was better known?'
   'Well,' I'm told, he stayed longer,
logging up the quantity, 'but class, all class belongs to you,
Henn.'
   Taa Wearney, who reckons I was 'fearless'.
I tell him I was bored. 'But,'
I need to add, 'we entertained them, didn't we...
after our fashion?'
      Everywhere I go I'm told
Weren't you one mad cunt, Bob!
Not quite, my friends. I was just the one to ask
Fearless? One day she'll all finish;
and after you fear that fear what fear remains?
   Col Bird, finished. Kidder, finished.
Tait, alive but finished. And who was that couple?
Anyway finished. The dumber drugs, the more ridiculous cars,
and those dumber, more ridiculous clowns
you meet on South Yarra station.
Not Lew-Fatt though. When you're those equal parts
smart-arse and crazy you finish when you want to.
Whilst out at Lilydale Johnny simply marinates
in what his current dealer brings around. Dunno
Hannaford's lesson, but he learnt it.
My lesson? Dunno mark two:
something to do with dope, no doubt not enough
of it.
   'Can you imagine,' I am asking Wearney,
'skinheads doing, really doing any kind of dope
with hair like that?'

'What hair?' says he.
If they've some kind of Mussolini complex,
either that or head lice
be his guest.
   Correct.
We grow it we have it, we have it we grow it.

    *

   And then, this warmish winter day in mid-July,
here at the corner of Orchard Grove and Canterbury Road
(territory I haven't really known since school)
Wearney invites me to his Thirtieth.
   'Thanks my friend, but not if I'm in Kathmandu.
Kathmandu and beyond.'
    'So,' he asks, 'when you were purged...'
    'Purged?' I answer.
       'You, Johnny and Hannaford,'
he replies, 'what was it you were on?'
   'On?' I'm asking, 'On? Back then?
Pancakes my friend, we were making pancakes.
Our very own 1963 drug of choice.
What other drugs were *back then*?
Doing the FBI a favour we asked ourselves
How can we best contribute to the place?
Obvious: don't turn up, make pancakes.'
   'So much for drugs,' says Wearney.
'What about that girl? Some place? Some cupboard?'
(And I see that now he's getting to it.)
'Yes where else would you hide when raided by
the FBI?'
    'Correct, my friend.'
   'And some other guy? Wasn't there
that other guy?'
    'Oh doesn't *Proper Gander* know
there always is?'

    *

Last time I saw Wearney I was twenty,
and didn't know it then but my days of
wearing Little Kim's sarong were fast collapsing.
Here though was a plan: she was going to climb
on my machine and we, the Kim 'n' Henn Show
would leave it, all of it: dole, debts, cops, folks
and end where we would end. (That's what I told him,
Wearney, one evening just across the road.)
           Then within a month a week,
a jack is telling me: '...think you're something, son?
Well actually...' and we all know how
that slow poncy word can take its time to hit
its target, 'actually, if nothing's something
Hendrickson, you're something haha get it?'
       Well God, for I found myself with little left to do
but summon him, my God, *whoever trawled the bottom-of-what*
to give us that one, I know enough of you
to know when we have both been had:
their pious stunts, that full-*collapse, your walking away.*
Which I can't do now.
                     'And if I'm nothing...'
But my reply paused, and it'll remain paused;
could've moved into some kind of *You'll keep* mode,
but who needs to sound like his Old Girl's God?
       Though I'll keep remembering what I might've said:
And if I'm nothing, I'm nothing like you.
Which has to be a great start.

                              *

       It's a light grey weekday afternoon,
about us the soft, slight hum of the suburb.
Like when Little Kim was settling behind, circling her arms
around
and we were moving off, I'm believing again,
knowing my life is set for even better living.
       So Wearney's told:
'Until we meet once more, go on, like I told you,
write my memoirs.
Now though, this arvo it's down the Peninsula,

say bye-byes to the Old Girl before I hit Nepal.
I've a date with some of their weirder shit
to help me grow an extra head, reckon it's deserved;
more dreams and even better memories,
aren't they anybody's extra head
and couldn't I be just anybody?'

                                        'Err,' goes Wearney,
'not whilst you're the star of *Operation Hendrickson*
and I'm the sole proprietor of *Proper Gander*.'
(And he's right and being right wants more.)
'Go on, give me a motto, your ever-essential
Henn motto.'

                    So three words fit, then four, five, six
and all is understood. '*Don't like it? Don't do it.*
For Wearney, that's what it's all about.'

Near Believing

The speaker is a former Anglo Catholic priest, now a Roman Catholic priest. He is married.

The Devil never tempts us with more success
than when he tempts us with the sight of our
own good actions.

Bishop Wilson

When I hosted *Sunday Evening with Father John,*
my producer, a most supportive sceptic
(and one I'd call a near-believer,
that kind of atheist I guess who prays at times)
gave as great a compliment as I'd received.
        'If you've taught me anything,' Rod confessed,
'it's this: the priesthood is no joke.'
        'True,' I agreed. 'Though what other occupation
ever had as great a scope for humour?
There you are, attempting to speak of, through and for
the Great Unknown himself, whilst every minute of
your spiel seems but another dare.
Let me see you'll ponder *if this time I can know,*
or more simply show, what I'm talking about,
truly talking about.'
                And if on Saturday evenings
that station's *Sexuality Show* was somewhat fatuous
(though for those times and on its terms well meaning)
often it seemed we both were giving
differing answers to quite similar questions.
If they, as an example, grasped for their latest
pop-psychology nostrums, there I'd be
relying on the staunchest of my standbys:
'Somewhere in Scripture, friends, I'm sure
we'll find an answer...' One day apart,
complimenting each other, talkback amateurs
counselling both questing and confused,
trying to explain in terms that Rod,
my honest and discreet (if sceptical) producer
might appreciate.

If I'd a mandate then
(we'll say I had) now I require a different one,
preparing me to give such answers as are necessary
to counsellor or advocate or friend,
certain there will be some flaws I might confess,
others offered as apologies and when required
others for evaluation or negotiation or denial.
      To someone I'll admit that then
I was a fool, a young fool, somewhat needing help;
to someone else how, though I acted simply
as myself, this still remains an issue:
that adolescent's crush on Father John;
whilst to a third let's be announcing thus:
She was and she still is a liar.
            And after my admissions have been understood
you'll find me quite light-headed,
knowing I could've been one greater fool
(though I wasn't) and now older, this shall find me
better for it.
                  Yes, I'll have myself concur, *the flaws…*
but in those days I was domiciled in a cobbled Faith,
one where a group of men stood in shadows,
near-believing something might exist beyond.
And though I've left such shadows
(who knows how God has told me but he's told me)
someone is still required, honest and discreet,
who'll still believe me, who'll have to understand
what we can, can't, must and mustn't say
beyond the room we're in.
Though prayers and sacraments shall help, that day
I won't be after judgement or redemption.
My crisis will have arrived (as Pamela and I both understand
it will) and I'll be found talking to, yet through,
another man's honesty and discretion, so that this once
I might hear myself, trusting we both understand
(as I hoped that producer would) and then believe.
      'What a natural at this you are!'
Rod would further compliment. 'Even if you hardly knew
you were…'
            And there I'd be,

confronted by my Sunday evening ranters,
urgent for doses of the hottest gospelling,
when mine were more designed to be lukewarm.
Bland does it Father John,
you haven't yet acquired a gift for public mayhem.

      So all I could allow myself was more pretence:
imagining I could interrupt this hyper-evangelist,
that God-denier with *Thanks my friend thanks heaps…*
now though we pause…pause for a word from our sponsor…
then swing in with the 'Hallelujah Chorus'.

                           And Leo,
for all his very few, flamboyant priestly years,
would have had that touch.

      At College Leo Pengilly, Geoff Cattermole and I
became that kind of coterie made for overreaching.

      'I mean,' mused Leo, 'how high can we Anglo Catholics fly
before we jet to Rome?'

            More though at ground level,
plenty of weekday nights in we'd tune for
Garner Ted Armstrong's *The World Tomorrow,*
our special *Can you believe this?* moment,
from someone never quite the enemy (to me at least)
more a form of very mad and very distant relative
you felt proud to tolerate.

            Though now I'm asking:
'Who today might be so tolerant of Father John, his Pamela
and the truth?'

      I found her first, my girl that I would marry,
as dumpy yet serene. And looking at her
(for God indeed was telling me to look)
I was informing 'Lord, I shall attend to Pamela…'
and telling myself (if a touch less godly)
'When all her puberty and adolescence ceases
then we'll marry.'

      True nowadays this asks belief.
And if it requires a logic, as in Our Lord's logic,
it'll be one sure to invite the sceptics.
Though there are those like that producer
who seem so poised at the edge of belief,
and I'd rather them than plenty of my talkback

congregation.

        For even then I knew their kind,
that kind who have decided
One day you'll be finished Father John
and all they had to do was wait, decades if required,
for anybody with her tale to tell,
part of her tale to tell, or part of her tale
heard or overheard to tell.
 I know it's believed I did what many young men did
and God has always known this. But if I'm asked
'Is there, John, any need for counselling?'
'More,' I'll reply, 'a need for relevant solicitors.'
        And if such bravado doesn't exactly jell with
many an idea of God or a man of God, let's reiterate:
Father John is for Our Lord and Pamela:
they saw him through his ministries, radio evenings
and columns in *The Sunday Press*; his publications;
their three daughters; T*he Good Shepherd Foundation,*
The Bio-ethics Centre and his *Friends of Life*;
his conversion and Pamela's conversion,
when all remaining shadows that surrounded both of them
dissolved, to be crowned, crowned by his re-ordination.
For without God, without Pamela, how could you, Father John,
achieve your culmination, this College that you founded,
where Western thought and Western arts
wedded to our eternal Faith would help produce such truth,
those far worse than the merely sceptical never will
forgive you.
        And based on that, all that,
I'll be at least allowed to say
(for I'm becoming quite their target)
If what occurred did, what never occurred
did not.
        As a vocation aren't we as priests in some sense
naked, with so much of society slouched
in the front row perving up?
        You may have read of this example:
let's say you've been swimming and, in the changing rooms,
under the showers, there he is, the nation's favourite ·
fair game cleric (and yes he has to be a bishop!).

It must take a near-to-carnal joy when you recall
how he was recognized and told
'I know what you're up to...piss off from here...
if you return I'll call the cops!'
        This man, this naked and derided bishop
I understand him. It isn't me, it never was,
but may as well be.
                That's what I'd confess,
since if I 'got away', I 'got away' with little,
so little heading nothing.
                    And you must understand
that yes it's no mistake how Pamela and this other lass
possessed a crush on me: the short, stocky thirteen-year-old,
her tall, thin fourteen-year-old friend,
whom I always liked (even if she never had
that preternatural serenity of Pamela)
who always knew I'd never marry her,
who four decades on lopes in:
some tall, if not so thin, middle-aged sexologist
wishing all the good that I've seen done,
the Foundations, Centres and my very College
turn redundant. *Piss off from here* indeed.
        But when you're young, bustling and with yes
plenty hidden behind that bustle,
when you are not just 'in charge', much more
you are this very one required to be 'in charge',
isn't that almighty potent?
                  These maxims helped:
Love the sinner hate the sin;
Weigh that good one may do beside that bad
one may have done. And if (from such) dilemmas
are discovered, please appreciate: out of these dilemmas
grow much of your true power.
                    Trust though
I've never lied to God. When I confess
there's you, there's your confessor,
there's God. Need there be more?
        And mightn't one write it off so many times
as simply 'sex'? One might if all such 'sex' isn't so removed
from what is written of, what is talked about:

'sexuality-sex'.

Consider these nuances,
assume that there's a girl with a crush on you,
on Father John, who leaps into your lap.
You're supposed to announce 'Get off my lap, girl!'
But for an under-experienced man
what should or shouldn't happen happens.
Fourteen or not she knows what's there,
what accident has occurred.

Consider the first time someone brushes
an arousal. Then ask *Is their virginity over?*
Something may very well be over,
for plenty this might be quite rightly frightening,
others much less so, since something dark
must have informed such girls *I did that
and no-one else.* They're young but they're participating:
there's fourteen-year-olds who do,
fifty-four-year-olds who never will.

What's a name appropriate to those times?
Let's make her Toni (Pamela's friend).
Toni embarking on her shy yet artful pranks,
Toni understanding *It's happening with a priest!*

Though I've been reconciled,
some days I may still think and care about it,
how both of us felt mighty awkward and were,
wouldn't one like to believe, near equals?

But Toni with her Toni crush continues.
And if it modifies at times, draws back, it then resurges,
for one day there will be no stopping Toni.
And wouldn't I love to have such power which says
Please, please, all these pranks must cease
except what Toni's offering seems needed,
and I think of all the good I'm set to do
once such current needs have been disposed.
(Besides there were such joyous days when Toni
wasn't needed!)

Prayer helped. I prayed for Toni, Pamela, myself,
those I was helping and would help.

And, if one supposes I demanded
truly demanded Toni for her help,

few would have served more willingly.
(I'm sure some Communist may have been more restrained.
Now there's a pure, ground-level faith and power
which only God can save.)
   'Come here…' I may have suggested, only suggested
or hardly that.
     So we'd look at each other, nod,
and you know Toni's type *Let's hint it dirty to a priest,*
tell things we'd never even tell the girlfriends,
these should get him rigid.
   She had me. After a year then onto two,
three, four, all Father John need do is to nod his nod
and off they'd go, him and Toni bound to where their nod
was heading. And mightn't you say how her crush
required it? Of course we both required it now,
for the intensity of my priestly bustle rose and rose
following every time with Toni, knowing how steadier
I was turning, to do much better than any
merest 'good'. Besides, I'd Pamela.
   For soon I'd be requiring someone I could tell
(if hardly brag) to Leo, Geoff or even God, how
Yes, my Pamela, the one I chose was thirteen when we met…
yet we were sure it was set to last…
   Even if there was that early time:
each of them seated on a knee,
with my eyes closed and ear-drums thudding
to our heartbeats.
     We were young,
two of us were very young, all doing silly things.
Though weren't there accidents, let alone mysteries
to solve, that thirteen-year-olds, fourteen-year-olds
and even priests require solving?
And if the priest wasn't Father John, plenty more
would be much worse.
   Toni was as I've indicated tall,
getting netballer taller now, and I'd to keep my head down,
if slightly down, not quite looking up at her,
knowing what needed to be said.
     At the seaside,
whilst she and I paced the length of the strand,

I tried explaining, not in sermon terms,
nor talkback terms, but terms for a teenage girl
with her over-extended crush: 'Let's stop, please.
I'll be wedding someone else one day. Thanks for understanding.
Hardly an hour elapses when I'm not announcing
Sorry if you feel I used you Toni, I understand,
I used myself and my vocation.'
                                        She isn't set to cry is she?
No, she's going to wait and wait until my work,
my true Lord's work is set to culminate.
Then back she blunders, poised to stymie,
this fifty-four-year-old sexologist who should've known,
decades back, it needed ending.
                                        But there I was,
after driving Toni home heading to my digs
where, God be thanked for this one,
Pamela, my dumpy little Pamela awaited.
True she'd been thirteen once, but true I knew
how it would last and yes in asking God
I knew of his reply *You can't approach too much of this*
with logic, not a logic to be understood, don't try.
Father, approach through Faith.
            She's nineteen when we marry and at thirty-two
I don't believe I've compromised her.
Right from the age young women know such things
Pamela knew our love, knew it for no conventional
Twentieth Century romance (though what with
Twentieth Century priests ever proved conventional?).
            And if I'd never over-advertise
this remained a story to be proud of:
our peck-on-the-cheek courtship
(well more than that if hardly more)
which mightn't be the way the world ran its affairs
(though you must love the sinner hate the sin)
but for us it seemed natural as Creation.
            Leo adored the idea of High Victorian
priestly rectitude and Geoff admired let's say
the tale, eyebrows rising as he muttered what
I can't recall.
                    'If this isn't,' Leo proffered,

'quite my way of tackling things,
how though did you do it?'

Her brother for best man
the Dean married us, and there in the back pew,
now filled up and out towered Toni, uninvited,
nodding.

And of course we had to laugh
at this young priest announcing,
in those hours prior to his nuptial night,
'I think I know what I'm doing!'

We all try to.
Long past his active priesthood, Leo
(ESL teacher, bon homme reprobate)
cruises and picks up some fine-moustached,
olive-toned young man. After they have done
what must be done Leo asks his age.
Fourteen. The boy leaves, Leo doesn't sleep and
in a measured panic Geoff is phoned at breakfast.
'Cattermole,' is heard, 'last night I did this
very silly thing.'

And though the boy told later how he'd been up for such
over the past few years, fourteen wasn't Leo's style,
or so he thought.

Geoff, who rather envies Leo's way
of plunging into what the flesh can offer,
knows his worldly-wisdom's under threat.
You hardly scold a friend of course and no, Leo,
you shouldn't have been up for it,
but since you were what is the chance
this will occur again?

'Next time,' chides Geoff,
'ask for an ID. Yes there are excuses and one day
such excuses probably won't hold;
though till then shut up and pray, Leo, pray
he won't resurface.'

Fourteen? Fifteen? Sixteen?
Sometimes I sensed Pamela was near-bursting
to try out something (like when she and Toni
cornered me in that crush) though soon of course
God I'm sure taught her his better way,

to simply wait till I'd be hers.

Sixteen? Fifteen? Fourteen?

Parts of me remain there.
Take my boyhood in 'Colin Thiele Land',
with its illegal silo-climbing, small town scouting,
our bemusing friends the Lutherans,
my own regime of prayer to keep
the world, the flesh and the Devil at bay.
Though how could you fault that lust of worship
emanating from the Lutherans?

I never could receive
those skewed gifts that they received
(not slightly-churchie me) nor those of the hyper-
churchie *Inter School Christian Fellowship.*
Yet I'd acquired limits, in that town you had to,
for at fourteen here's what's understood:
what really happens happens behind doors,
doesn't it? It will, though everybody knows
the latest pregnancies on show, whose face
looks bruised, what scout master has left town.
In a place that size you cannot dissolve
into a nearby suburb, what's done remains that
ever present done, and if you're dumb enough to yell
'Piss off!' at some teacher, next time she sees you
isn't she coming out of Foodland? Not that it was me
who did, young John had found his limits.

As Father John found his.
Had I sympathy for any sinner? Yes of course,
unless he was our Sunday School boss and all fool
Mr L.G. Baker, who sprung in his car with that
fifteen-year-old, needed to quit our parish.
Yes for some there might be a certain tragedy,
hearing this florid Englishman huffing-on:
'What are you saying? I wish to be informed, sir!'

No Mr L.G. Baker it's Saint Augustine's, us,
who's wishing for the information.

And yes, I suppose it was difficult for
our vestry to yield much sense re you and your
young girl except that 'Gentlemen…'
lapsing into my most theatrical I didn't care,

'Gentlemen…it's a boy!'
To which they never yielded any sense.
　　　　Does Our Lord pray?
　　　'Father John,' I liked to believe I heard him,
'there's works, good works and very good works
for us to do. With Pamela quite ready now
we needn't go Mr L.G. Baker's way, now need we?'
　　　　With reason plus the aid of Faith I believed
we needn't.
　　　　　　Still there'd been months when,
evening or night or late night, draped in mufti
I'd seek out the parklands.
If, with no Toni now, somethings may've got a touch
too grubby, please understand,
with only briefest phrases for the latest Mr. Wrong
and no penetration, I wasn't set to discover how
the other half ruts.
　　　　　　'It's this,' I'd tell them,
'my fiancé, who doesn't know I'm here,
wishes, as I am wishing too, that she's remaining
(get this one boyo!) ready. I've also had this girl friend who…'
　　　　These men I was soon to learn
were never there for any justifying, simply though
to do it, do it as Toni did quite readily her sordid,
very necessary mission.
　　　　　　　'So, apart from this,'
they might ask, 'what else might you do…'
ask as we ambled from the parkland.
I was this kind of chaplain if you must, a priest.
　　　　And during that chaplaincy,
when as a young man attending plenty of young man issues
(those hidden, those less-than-hidden)
a somewhat younger man is in my office
filled with fantasies (please don't pause to guess)
of other young men. And needing help to just find out
who he is or what he is, Father John's required
to respond.
　　　　We'll make him Tony, T-o-n-y Tony,
and I've often thought I might've liked him
much the way I always liked the other Toni.

But haven't you had such moments:
Why am I hearing this? or its oops! twin
Never should've said that...should I?
This was my moment: with T-o-n-y seeing me
some co-conspirator and/or victim, the day belongs
to Father John who, having heard enough, won't be
holding back.
              'Sometimes matey,' as I matey'd him,
'please feel, believe and know there's little more
beloved by God than sinners.
So understand that sinner in yourself and soon,
once you've the head and heart and guts enough
you'll binge, regret and yield to binge once more.
It's something I've learnt (as you'll learn it too)
for few can sin as a priest can sin. Plus this:
when you hint it dirty, what's a priest to do?
Hint it extra dirty in return?
Well go on and hint hint hint,
just don't coup de grâce me thus:
how you're married to some nothing girl
who just lies there. Make up that tortured,
young man's mind and better yet get right out
and cruise, cruise with all your fellow sinners, Tony.
After which if you require forgiveness, forgiveness
will await!'
              Let's say I told him that and
whatever version constitutes the rest,
the excitement can be grasped, can't it?
I won't say it was exactly 'good', yet hadn't I done well,
saving something honest in that sinner,
giving a dull young man something to sin about?
              'Getting nervy?' I'd to ask him.
'I'm no holy-roller, boyo . Father John just overbrims
with Friar Tuck good fellowship, who'd even thrash you,
if you wished, Tony you tiresome tease.
We both know why you're here,
and I could have you, have you enough to say
I've had him! to whoever cares.
But I've good news: there's plenty of that other
non-penetrative stuff you can escape with,

confess as you need or needn't,
as it's the sinner gets redemption, never sin.'

And hardly wishing much to happen,
I placed an arm around the shoulders of
this boring boyo, an act so accidental I was shocked.
Though truly, if I was guilty mine was the guilt of anger,
an anger to hate enough both Tony and his 'sins'.

Try asking in the middle of the middle of
middle Australia after the good I did
and none shall ever be aware (nor need they)
of that temptation deluge which can confront
even their best of priests.

Have you read:
Termination: A Woman's Tragic Choice,
or *In Response with Father John*?
If you have, mightn't you understand how so much
could absolve me?

Or consider this:
with Pamela wanting to teach, we prayed for her
and so she taught, how could she not?
More than even mine, if less that God's,
Pamela was her own true woman.

Indeed she was. After our daughters arrived
she developed tricks, such beautiful, fulfilling
love-tricks, those I can hear sexologists announce
I've ordered her perform, the kind they think commence
Come, leap into my lap, child...

And as we got older, stronger, more exciting
they became. Then, whilst she chose something from
her repertoire I'd find myself confiding
'If only Saint Augustine's knew...'
and she'd snigger, how I loved her snigger.

She'd suggest we listen to *The Sexuality Show*.
'Haven't you, 'I asked, 'got enough ideas?'

She laughed, I always shall enjoy that laugh but
'When did we begin all this?' she posed.

How did she mean?

'When?' she replied.

When did she think?

And then

she had to mention Toni, Toni and us.
Was this a dare? Was she understanding something
that she needn't?
                              'John,' no snigger, no laugh,
this was just a smile, 'John we had all that,
and now we have all this. Haven't we always had our Faith
and God?'
              For as with her love she'd always known
that when Faith is lost the warping starts,
and from those warps surge in a sweep of trends:
'faith' being 'relevant', 'faith' being 'contemporary',
Our Lord as good guy.
                              And it's then she knows,
 we know, her Father John is ready,
hardly that wishy-washy radio priest admired
by his producer.
              Always poised to see a certain kind of sceptic ambushed,
'Let's start,' he asks, 'let's start with birth control.'
              (A male is sure to look bewildered;
females may arise and leave the room.)
                              'Correct,'
says Father John, 'with birth control.
As if Creation ought to be controlled. Or this:
that Faith should never take on science.
Why yes it should…' (Again they're caught.)
'Faith,' they need to have explained,
'may well be right, for Faith has driven me, you, us
and them far further than mere science can.
If you're hearing me because of Faith
(that sceptic's faith which God I'm sure
has given you) it is because one part of your brain,
mind and even soul has faith enough to ask
Getting it wrong…isn't he?
              No matter how many empires over-reach and fall
Faith yet remains. And to purge through Faith, my Faith,
all the mess that empires make of God's own word
and world, even if that purging's just that smallest good
I've tried to do, is what I'd love to tell them,
love to tell you too, Toni.
              How often must I rehearse and even pray

such lines? As many times as I've been stymied.
Soon as you show you're more than mere parochial,
it truly starts: *Let's ask Father John,*
let's hint heresy to the celebrity-priest.
It's then you'd find me: stared by yet staring down
The Harpies.

       'Women,' I urged them, 'trust me please.
I've never taken what you believe for *heresy*,
but if it were doctrine, true and unadorned
with spiritual foundations, wouldn't I be first
to back your ordinations? But it isn't, I cannot and
I will not. Approaching God is difficult enough,
who needs that extra hair shirt?'

          Like Pamela?
My wife in their sights, you knew they thought it:
See those daughters he's been given, hear that ardour
she's supplied.

      And some might say I will run from that,
that kind of *that*, to hide in Rome,
as if Rome would permit mine or any hiding.
For when you feel so closer to the Saviour,
you are hardly hiding, but it's your business,
his business, no-one else's and surely not
The Harpies.

      We're in our final year at
Saint Augustine's, and very soon I'm to be told
where I'll be heading. Later it's not so strange having us ask
'Was God speaking to us through that harridan?'
and answer 'Maybe he was.'

      In Melbourne for *The Cross Denominational Commission*,
I co-chair with Pastor Bob Van Hoof,
he says one thing, I reply with another,
everyone prays.

      Geoff would love to meet me,
assures how Leo, our wicked-to-the-point-of innocence
clerical drop out would love meeting me too.
Bring the Pastor? Why not bring the Pastor.

      So there are seven for an alcove at *Sotto Voce*,
Geoff's local pasta place: Pamela, myself, Leo,
Leo's faghag, the Cattermoles, Van Hoof.

Acting as hosts we ask Van Hoof for grace,
and all seems settled for good-food-and-wine-time,
till über-Harpy Bess Cattermole implodes,
this thoroughly modern, very Protestant implosion.
    Bess hardly liked me and,
with all necessary fellowship under stress,
I've hardly liked her too. Tonight, from opposite ends
of everywhere we're rounding on the other,
and on birth control, divorce, termination and
on life itself, plus certain trends I fear shall lead
into a form of un-Australian disbelief.
She would like to be ordained, I would like to put a clamp
on her fishwifery. Didn't Bess understand
those more important issues, those most disturbing warps
occurring in the fabric of our Faith and nation,
though with this necessary rider...
                        'Don't tell, John,'
she sneers, 'love that sinner, hate that sin!'
Then exposing us her unhappy clappy self with
'Just piss off to Rome!' she runs out howling
to the Ladies. So much for sotto voce.
    The women folk heading off to soothe her,
I'm sweating, Geoff's mumbling, Leo's seeped in
his drug of choice, whilst Van Hoof just stares.
Poor Van Hoof: the hyper-churchiest son of our
home town, few could be happier and clappier
than Pastor Bob. On liturgy, on doctrine,
we never shared a single path to part from,
we merely waved our ecumenical waves
backing the other for a good, good man.
    Though as Australians well aware of warps,
warps and their inevitable trends,
Father John and Pastor Bob frequently coincide.
Best not tell Bess.
        A further Harpy:
weeks on see Pamela and I driving from
a concert or the theatre, and there,
first time on *The Sexuality Show*, in her measured,
humanist, counselling mode meet Toni,
telling us whatever she's been taught

Love the neurotic, reconcile the neurosis. Yes Toni,
with all those consenting adults tuning in,
the girl who once had loved and reconciled so much
for Father John, since you're to note, re-note,
and understand how young we were:
a third of me (no more) crazed by her pranks yes,
but two thirds plus so devoted to my Pamela.
(Would that I could reconcile *You were loved,*
not just for what you were doing, Toni
with all that ugly near-believing joy
she had me feel.)

          How much belief remains
as near-belief? *That* a Leo or a Geoff might say
is as much as you'll achieve.

          Yet the more I heard myself or even better
heard God through myself, the more that this
was known: name the resources, Rome would have them,
my issues as their issues as our issues,
then add such expertise which I might bring.

          Had changing sides been easy?
Though Leo now had blundered into Heaven,
Geoff remained, taking such changes with detachment,
plus undoubted prayers to temper my conversion.

          Later when I was ordained he was invited
and accepted. Pamela aside few knew how far
Father John had travelled.

                    We embraced.

          'Fully crossed the Tiber?'
And that was Geoff, sympathetic yet bemused.
'What a long, long way around, how did you ever
do it?'

          Though I wonder what he made of
my prelate's ordination sermon, how
'As witnesses to chastity, in such a sex-obsessed society,
celibates have their primal place.
Though now God's sent this other kind of priest,
to give a different witness, one to correct such sceptics
as assail our Faith, with all their *Ho ho ho,*
what would they *ever know?*'

                (What would I know ho ho?

God knew I knew too much, knew how far I'd go,
we all might go.)
His Grace turned,
to grasp me by the shoulders:
'This will be,' (by now we both were staring straight
into the other) 'a double coup,' he celebrated.
'For us your expertise, for you your dispensation.
Speak, John. Speak out upon the joys of marriage,
speak out and be believed.
You will be withering.'
'And Pamela?' I asked.
'Yes Pamela indeed. Our Faith and nation
need such witnesses.'

The Sexuality Show still has its witnesses.
Now run by Toni it will never cease.
And every week you'd see us poised to hear
further of her flaky nostrums, till I'm crying
Wow Toni, do you believe such stuff?
Yet it enchants this hokum. Until we hear her
starting on the Toni story, how
'Yes, at a young age I too was taken, taken by one
who in his field became most eminent.'
Well *Wow Toni*, I adore the way
that must've been rehearsed for decades,
no names of course, but as elaborations multiply
anyone with a tabloid disposition
can get the hints and link the hints
till Toni's near enough believed.

But I'm believing too, believing *Wow Toni.*
They were, as you are quite aware, mutual,
mutual pranks and accidents. Now though,
quitting such small town stuff I, my Faith and Church
are set to found our College, well away from you.

And if such Saturdays had turned truly bad
please guess what Sundays were becoming,
when what replaced me seems like some
Uniting Church mum.

But then that Sunday night,
just before we leave to found my College,
hearing such humanist fag-ends of what purports to be a Faith,

I need my corrective, and have to think again of Toni,
recalling just how much she grew to love, not merely the idea
but the thrill of Father John's marvelling sobs
Wow, aren't you amazing! For when that happened
she would turn so proud.

       And I might admit to plenty more,
but wouldn't that destroy such necessary good
we've been sent to do?
I've no desire to let the prurient
I know what you're up to…piss off from here…
swoop down on those who may have been weak once
(I should never revel in my weaknesses then but
how weak I was!) plus that ruthless gunning for
the off off-limits of Pamela and our Faith.

       And yet if they want ruthless let's give it:
too many have been called by the tabloids and replied
(too many have been called by God and never replied).
Whilst this shall be their unforgiving
tabloid doctrine: *Your onetime hierarchy knew,*
as your present hierarchy knows (good career move,
Father John) that you were and doubtless shall remain
predatory, deceitful and a hypocrite.

       Well he's not asking *Who isn't?* Nor does he suggest
some statute of moral limitations,
but if you believe that all, all of it occurred
please prove same, you'll never hear my damming
guilt-in-protestation like Mr L.G. Baker's
plaintive blusters.

       My Pamela won't sigh that often,
but there's the day I'm hearing
'Why must this be brought up *now?*'

                Why?
Because we understand they want us destroyed,
it's you, I, God and and all who back us ranged against
those who'll never wish to understand.

       Hadn't we waited till Pamela was set,
both of us were set? We needn't have.
There was that time I too 'updated' 'faith',
brought 'relevance' to 'contemporary youth',
your good guy in the rectory.

And if that Toni mess had unravelled then?
If she'd found someone to believe her?
Then such belief would turn into a tabloid
hunting party: young Father John as quarry.
        From pre-conception to well past the grave,
how many give such a support to life as priests?
You not merely befriend, let alone counsel,
you rescue, reconcile sinners with their Lord and Saviour,
and if at times the world outside our Faith
recoils from words as these, 'Lord' and 'Saviour' remain,
words which have much more than mere 'survived'.
(Can we be sure 'sexologist' will see a decade out?)
        Please shred all cant and ask:
who walked off each time fulfilled and proud,
and who had his career, vocation, life and even soul
at stake? She knew the pranks and accidents on offer,
whilst I was offering what? That a priest, as any man,
is many men.
                So try imagining as I do, this one:
how the girlfriend's dad grabs at the boyfriend's throat,
ramming his head into a wall. Couldn't that be your head,
yet couldn't you be that dad? Yes we are many men.
        Let's though recall and fully believe in this:
once the Limousine drove up and His Eminence strode into
our College, there would remain no happier occasion.
        'Father,' he beamed, 'so much of this edifice
is yours and always will be.'
                        'From here, Eminence,'
I couldn't be contained since this was indeed
our day for beaming, 'it's from here we will
engage them!'
                And he understood just who I meant
and how I meant it.
                    Except I'd three months left.
        Thanks to that tabloid
(the same which used to promote their Father John)
Sunday upon Sunday now, I became their two-faced fraud-defiler,
for there are lies, there are tabloid lies, and then there are
sexologist lies.
        Leaving all to lower clerics His Eminence

wouldn't have to see me. Allowing how
it's better for the Faith he never has.
He knows what lies are like.

       For after Toni's re-emergence,
and those other women-women-women
I've hardly met, enter Mr Coup de Grâce himself
T-o-n-y Tony.

       Who's left to even near-believe me?
Leo, once? Except the story Leo knew
was one I wished him to believe. Geoff?
Since his wife has disembarked on Lesbos
Bishop Cattermole's hooked-up, and I mean hooked,
with a certain lady vicar.

       Whilst to those I've joined in my most
sincerest act of Faith, doubtless I'll appear as double-damage,
someone washed ashore who's brought to Rome
an unwelcome variant of their current plague.

       There's only Pamela, perhaps our daughters,
and you Lord you, through whom I'll hear my truth
(an 'unofficial' one alas, compared to all the growing
more 'official' ones).

       And Toni? It wasn't that she lost a faith
she rarely had, rather it was Father John, wasn't it,
who turned her sceptic and sexologist?
How were we to know each would prove that pivot upon which
so much of our later lives revolved?
If only she had been some, mythic, broad-beamed,
housewife-masseuse, my lapse in priestly taste.
Instead she must remain another of their
less-than-proven fantasies:
that sweet, young, not-exactly-filled-out girl,
and few will understand how unfair that is,
given my work lies in atonement,
an atonement Toni may not know of, though you do
don't you Lord?

          Regret? That I never explained that part of
my life to Geoff or Leo? To Leo with all his drug-fug
penetrative madness? To Geoff?
The man who thinks he knows the lot
would need informing 'Ah no you don't!'

Let me be adept enough explaining this:
here was a girl I sought to trust, and better
believed I could; as when we met Pamela and I
soon trusted we would be one day as one,
though I was twice her age.

      And if Leo and Geoff moved on to
(let's be blunt) hardly some 'City of Churches',
Father John remained, ministering to his parched,
straight-lined town, knowing he'd be near-enough
believed (as, when he returns, we're sure to hear
such catalogues of disbelieving).

      Ready to believe some better news?
It may be late news (we were at Saint Augustine's then)
but when we were presented to Her Majesty
(and even if she had been briefed)
'Ah Father John,' I rather felt she glowed,
'our radio priest and his good lady...'
Which was gracious, she never had to say it,
but then she's mentioning *The Good Shepherd Foundation*,
and maybe soon, had she heard, a bishopric?

      'Soon Ma'am?' I stammered and I knew
I stammered. 'Only God for certain knows.'
(Poor woman surely hears a lot of stammering.)

      'And his good lady!' Hours after Pamela too
was glowing. 'Delightfully old fashioned,
like we were imagined by George Eliot...'

      Perhaps we were, though hardly subscribing to
such modes of High Victoriana as were Leo's.
Here's his vision (brilliant, camp-preposterous,
utterly out-of-time) of parenthood:
how each evening he'd receive his daughters,
Dido and Ariadne, running in to lisp
their Latin and their Greek declensions,
just before they toddled off to bed.
(And Leo's gag so blended with his vision
you felt, thought and knew his near-belief!)

      'Instead,' sneered Geoff, 'he ended in St Kilda,
smoking dope and sucking cocks!'

      And maybe it's where God sent him,
for though I'd hardly mention such in any sermon

God can be delightfully profane.
Shouldn't he be asked? We often do.

      Really John and I can hear Pamela, glowing
as she always has *really!*

                For despite the Tonis and
the Tonys and the Bess Cattermoles,
we can justify ourselves to ourselves and God
far more than many. And whilst the College
can expunge just as it deems, so much of their edifice
is mine. (Pamela and I both heard those words,
such eminent words which shall remain.)

      We think of 'it', that Toni 'it', most days,
but reconciling 'it' we've got this far.
(How often are you expected to believe all 'it'
truly happened?)

          And of course,
since every sordid word of 'it' has now been written down
and plastered up, we'll sue.

Press Play

Will't please you sit and look at her?
                    Browning

That's her! Admit it, this shot sure is sweet,
you've but to ask we'll switch into *Repeat*
or simply *Pause* until *Play* is pressed.
It's beyond mere business given you're my guest
and here's the evidence, *Playtime* on my screen,
of who she was, who she might have been:
I'm what you want and I'm supplying plenty...
        For what girl looked more tempting circa Twenty?
They term it 'adult'? 'Innocence' sounds better,
ripe to be rescued, the moment that I met her,
from all that sweaty tackiness which went
with long-lunching middle-management,
bugs in suits not doing overmuch
but perving, panting, too afraid to touch.
(Shall we press *Pause* then *Play* then *Pause* again?)
She's waxed, enhanced with all these men men men
it's almost near an abattoir as pub.
        'So where on the food-chain do I notch you, grub?'
the DJ's asked. He'd mates, they somehow laughed
their near-appreciation of my craft,
to understand that whilst I play the loner
and she's a free agent, they would never own her.
Then, taking time to fine-tune my mission
I sensed correct, plugged into her ambition:
'If you've a goal so let's achieve that goal,
isn't life more than sliding round some pole?'
        For that's how this man beckons *You're the one...*
though please there is no secret why it's done,
as thugs demand or some deadshit begs
I just suggest, a reflex moves those legs.
        Next try to guess this target of my scorn,
those kinds of outbursts where the line gets drawn:
'Look at that scrubber, wadda ya reckon, Chief?'

And I'll recoil, for it isn't in our brief
to sneer at any hare-lip, any limp,
to play the preacher nor much less the pimp.
        We chose 'companions', 'escorts' sounding trite.
To see you through most days and any night
Select Companions for the rich enough,
with her our grandest asset, no excess puff
required: Miss Natural, top-of-the-range, prime.
        Until we hired her out to *Partytime*
and lacking caution, even more the smarts
is where a one thing stops, another starts.
For doubled then redoubled suppliers grew,
dealing on cue her now chaotic brew
of pharmaceuticals. Most have barely heard
their toxic vocab, word-upon-conjured-word;
as each new substance rules how a heartbeat chugs
let's baptise generations by their drugs.
        Whatever hers though somethings have to stop
and see me set to turn the workplace cop.
though not for Madam's backhanded tat-taa hiss:
'It's you,' she sneers, 'got me into this.'
        That life you loved or its entire botch?
Sweetheart accept this happened on your watch,
whilst there I viewed you near-verging as some wife...
but after those months of all that substance life,
of *Play/Pause/Play/Pause*...finally I *Fast-forward*
informing whoever matters. She's deported,
that's what I'm told. Now to view what's missed
pick up the remote and aren't I back-to-blissed,
as *Play* is pressed all she was remains.
        There have been losses, but outweighed by the gains,
as best intentions keep me out of hock,
most days are spent attending to my flock,
the giggling demur or the upfront teaser,
send one out shopping, get one her student visa.
Unlike that Taiwan crowd before the last
we're an outfit where the past stays in the past
to never make the headlines. Trust us. Any loss

much less embarrassment we'll bear. Inform your boss
I'll set a day to get us three acquainted.
(It's friendship first and then the deal, well ain't it?)
No qualms meanwhile in picking up her tab.

      Let's buzz the front desk, have them book a cab.

Notes

Eating Out
NIDA: Sydney based National Institute of Dramatic Art.
Bakeries: in the late 1960s certain Melbourne Maoists (Les Chinois) had their headquarters in a disused bakery.

Climbing up the Ladder of Love
Stabber Jack: one-time Labor term of abuse for a traitor, coined initially for politician Jack Beasley.
Toorak Times: Melbourne scandal sheet of the 1970s and 1980s.

Roger, or Of Love and its Anger
FRANZCP: Fellow of the Royal Australian and New Zealand College of Psychiatrists.

Down Under
The late 1970s, young Aussies in South-East Asia.
Harry Lee: Prime Minister Lee Kuan Yew of Singapore (1959-1990).
Terry Clark: leader of the New Zealand-in-origin Mr Asia Drug Syndicate, probably the most spectacular heroin importing combo in 1970s Australia.

It's Time
Motto and theme song of the Australian Labor Party's 1972 successful campaign after 23 years of Liberal-Country Party coalition rule.
Billy Bigears: Liberal Party Prime Minister William McMahon (1971-72).

On the Road to Gundagai
A family saga from the late 1950s to the time of writing. The song, a great singalong number was composed by Jack O'Hagan (1898-1987).

The Never Never
Brisbane in the 1930s and early 1940s as seen through the eyes of my mother's generation. This ballad by Letty Catts (something like a more austere Don't Fence Me In) became a big wartime hit.

A Brown Slouch Hat

My mother and her best friend join the army. The poem is dedicated to the best friend's elder daughter.

Deanna Durbin: my mother wrote a fan letter to Deanna and received a reply from the set of *Three Smart Girls*.

Eleanor Dark: popular Australian novelist.

Girls on the Avenue

A mid 1970s 'underground' black comedy on heroin addiction *Pure Shit*, was once described by John Forbes as the best ever Australian movie. He may still be right.

My Old Man's a Groovy Old Man

A young woman confronts the idea that her father has run off with her best friend.

Bound for Botany Bay

The television mini-series *Blue Murder* centres on the 'real life' relationship between Sydney underworld identity Arthur 'Neddy' Smith and rogue cop Roger Rogerson.

The Breakers: a dodgy police squad.

Sallie-Anne Huckstepp ('working girl'), her boy-friend Warren Lanfranchi (drug dealer) and Christopher 'Rentakill' Flannery (hit man) were all victims in the cop and criminal mayhem of 1970s and 1980s Sydney.

Kingsford-Smith: Sydney's major airport, on the shores of Botany Bay, is named after our most famous aviator Charles Kingsford-Smith.

In 1788 the British First Fleet, loaded with convicts landed in Australia, first in Botany Bay, then moving north to Sydney Harbour where they raised the flag and founded the eventual city.

A World of Our Own

1967, the upper middle class of suburban Melbourne.

The PM drowned: Liberal Prime Minister Harold Holt (1966-67) disappeared whilst skin-diving in rough surf.

I Go to Rio

The world of Peter Allen.

Frank and Ethel Gumm: grandparents of Liza Minelli Peter Allen's wife of a few years and parents of Judy Garland (Frances Gumm) his mother-in-law.

Carioca: pertaining to Rio de Janeiro.

Padre Pio: twentieth-century Italian friar, priest, stigmatist, and mystic.

The Maracana: Rio's famed football stadium.

PARE DE POR FAVOR MATAR NOSSOS CRIANCAS: from the Portuguese, 'Please stop murdering our children.'

Bad Habits

Hours before he heads off on an early morning flight to the U.S., a businessman has an escort visit his hotel room.

Love is in the Air

In 2040, the dedicatee, by now a woman of 30, watches film footage of her parent's wedding, where this song was played.

My Home Among the Gum Trees

Well known for its retention of native vegetation and indeed as a founding place for such urban conservation, Blackburn was my home suburb.

The Age or The Argus: Broadsheet newspapers.

'The King has died.' The death of George VI, my first memory of a public event.

Chatswood: Ruth Nash Speaks

The Bogle-Chandler case is one of the great Australian mysteries. Given that Bogle was a research physicist some believed he was murdered by the KGB/CIA/take your pick. For others, connections with wife-swapping Bohemia seems to indicate something else. In more recent times the toxic atmosphere arising from pollution of the Lane Cove River has been floated.

CSIRO: the Commonwealth Scientific and Industrial Organisation, the nation's peak body in that area. Bogle worked there as a scientist, Geoffrey Chandler as a photographer.

The God of Nope

Griffith: a town in south-west New South Wales, headquarters of the Calabrian Mafia's marijuana industry for many years.

Bircher: member of America's extreme right-wing John Birch Society.

Bernie: Bernie Houghton, CIA operative and Nugan-Hand associate who set up The Bourbon and Beefsteak, a bar in Sydney's King's Cross.

Buddy: U.S. Rear Admiral Earl 'Buddy' Yates, the Nugan-Hand Bank's president.

'Aussie Bob': Robert Trimbole (1931-1987) Griffith based organised crime figure, associate of both the Nugan-Hand Bank and the Mr Asia Drug Syndicate.

A High School Staff Room, Melbourne's Northern Suburbs, Winter 1977

Jim Cairns: Opposition to Australia's involvement in the invasion and occupation of Viet Nam was led by Labor MP Jim Cairns (1914-2003), later Deputy PM (1974-5).

E.T.: emergency teacher, i.e. supply or relief, term used in Victorian schools.

A Portrait of Three Young High School Teachers

Raymond Huntley: English actor from the 1930s to the 1980s who often played supercilious types in 1950s and 1960s British comedies.

Peace Congresses: convocations of a leftist bent occurring in the 1950s and 1960s, aiming at World Peace.

Revival Crusades: in the 1950s Oral Roberts and then Billy Graham visited Australia.

Breakfast with Darky

Sunnyside Up: television variety show.

Capitalist Roader: Maoist-inspired term of abuse.

Frank Hardy, Judah Waten and John Morrison were Social Realist writers.

Quadrant: right-wing intellectual magazine with a certain clout and even respect outside of the Right. Then not now.

They Came to Moorabbin

AWAS: Australian Women's Army Service in World War II.

Mr Menzies: Liberal Party Prime Minister 1939-1941, 1949-1965.

Goodbye Melbourne town, Melbourne town goodbye: references a 1907 Music Hall song.

HSV-7: Melbourne's first television station, which opened in 1956.

XVI Olympiad: held in Melbourne in 1956.

Yalumba: winery famous for its Sherry.

The Village Glee Club: radio program of the 1950s and 1960s.

IT'S ON AGAIN: tabloid billboard announcing the start of the Victorian Football League season.

Anger Management: a South Coast Tale

Leagues Clubs: Rugby League-sponsored clubs in New South Wales and Queensland devoted to eating, drinking, gambling and entertainment.

Bowlo: A lawn bowling club's premises devoted to eating, drinking, gambling and entertainment.

White Ox: roll your own cigarette tobacco.

AVO: Apprehended Violence Order: court order, quite often taken out against males in a domestic violence situation.

Waitin' for the Viet Cong

La Mama: alternative theatre/arts venue, located in inner-suburban Carlton since the mid-1960s.

Red Brick: any number of post-war British universities.

Operation Hendrickson

Winlaton: Local girls' reformatory.

Nasho: National Service selectively in operation 1964-1972.

Chick's Tech: technical high school for girls.

Markillies: flop-house hotel in the Melbourne CBD, now reconfigured for backpackers.

VCs: Viet Congs.

Patpong Rd: red-light area in Bangkok.

Crazy Horse. FucFuc: girly bar and tranny/gay bar in Bangkok. They first appeared in my verse novel The Lovemakers.

Bowater-Scott: paper towelling/toilet roll etc. manufacturer, with a factory in Box Hill South.

Burwood Tech: boys' technical high school.

King Gee: brand name of heavy-duty workwear.

Peninsula: Mornington Peninsula, holiday/retirement destination, 60-90 minutes south of Melbourne.

The Chase: shopping plaza.

Near Believing

ESL: English as a Second Language.

Colin Thiele: South Australian writer whose work often evoked the countryside and small towns of his state.

City of Churches: onetime nickname for Adelaide.

My thanks to the following who introduced, edited and published my poetry in book form or were agents thereof.

Public Relations: Martin Duwell

New Devil, New Parish: Frank Thompson and Roger McDonald

The Nightmarkets: Brian Johns and Jane Arms

Out Here (UK): Michael Heyward and Neil Astley

The Lovemakers, Book One, Saying all the Great Sexy Things: Fran Bryson, Bob Sessions and Heather Cam

The Lovemakers, Book Two, Money and Nothing: Fran Bryson, Stuart Neal and Carl Harrison-Ford

The Lovemakers (UK): Tony Frazer

The Australian Popular Songbook, *Prepare the Cabin for Landing* and *These Things are Real*: Ivor Indyk

The poem 'Near Believing' was first published in the journal *Antipodes* (Volume 33/Number 2)

And where do I start with those, particularly in the poetry community, who have backed my ambition and its outcomes? The list could be near-endless but for starters I would like to acknowledge the following: Paul Adams, Ken Bolton, Peter Craven, Jim Davidson, Laurie Duggan, Jas H. Duke, Martin Duwell, Annie English, John Forbes, John Hawke, Kris Hemensley, Luise Huck, Ivor Indyk, John Jenkins, Rae Desmond Jones, August Kleinzahler, John Leonard, Pi O, Nigel Roberts, Gig Ryan, John A. Scott, John Tranter and Chris Wallace-Crabbbe.

Michelle Borzi's unstinting editorial contribution I fully praise. Whatever my virtues let alone vices as a poet I'll never be an easy one to edit. Of course I did enjoy playing my part in the joint effort that was this project.

In 1985 the painter Jenny Watson produced a work inspired by *The Nightmarkets* [in manuscript]: portrait of a young woman looking into a mirror, who is I believe Sue Dobson, narrator of 'Climbing Up The Ladder of Love.' If the painting wasn't chosen for the book's cover, decades on a solid detail from it graces *Near Believing*. So many thanks to Jenny, the Roslyn Oxley9 Gallery, the University of Wollongong Art Collection, Grant Ellmers and Marius Foley who made this possible.

Certain of my monologues and narratives were simply too long to be included and it was decided that excerpts were no option. As an example there is the poem spoken by Eighties entrepreneur Craig Stubbs. Sorry Stubbsy but this time you just didn't make it.

And then there was the realisation that although the rogues galley which made up much of this selection contained plenty of its creator in these portraits, sometimes the poet's re-reading found him confronted with sections (albeit small) that had him announcing to his creations: 'Truly, this isn't *you* speaking…it's *me!*' Therefore such brief passages were excised.

Certain other poems, often being neither monologue nor narrative, have been deferred until *Based on Real Events*, a proposed Selected Light Verse; whilst there is a recently completed compilation of interconnected narratives set between 1913 and the near enough present day. (Did anyone mention verse novel?)

Readings by myself and Laura Munro now can be accessed via www.alanwearne.com.au. These comprise works recorded at the University of Wollongong for my Grand Parade Poets website; recorded by John Hawke for a CD featuring readings from *The Lovemakers*; and recorded by Jacqui Howarth for future use by the University Library. Plenty of these recitations are of poems appearing in *Near Believing*.

And finally, something to aspire to…

The predominant features of my music are passionate expression, inward intensity, rhythmic impetus, and a quality of unexpectedness.
Hector Berlioz